The Watchdog Still Barks

Beth Knobel

The Watchdog Still Barks

HOW ACCOUNTABILITY REPORTING EVOLVED
FOR THE DIGITAL AGE

FORDHAM UNIVERSITY PRESS · NEW YORK · 2018

Fordham University Press has no responsibility for the persistence or
accuracy of URLs for external or third-party Internet websites referred
to in this publication and does not guarantee that any content on such
websites is, or will remain, accurate or appropriate.

Fordham University Press also publishes its books in a variety of
electronic formats. Some content that appears in print may not be
available in electronic books.

Visit us online at www.fordhampress.com.

Library of Congress Cataloging-in-Publication Data available online at
https://catalog.loc.gov.

Printed in the United States of America

20 19 18 5 4 3 2 1

First edition

For the two remarkable men
whose impact on my life
has been invaluable:

Marvin Kalb
and
Mark Russell Shulman

CONTENTS

The Watchdog Still Barks

CHAPTER 1

The Watchdog Still Barks

I am a big fan of the comedian John Oliver, who often aims his edgy humor at important issues in American society. In August 2016, the object of his attention was the importance of watchdog journalism—the very subject of this book. In a nineteen-minute rant on his television show *Last Week Tonight* on HBO, Oliver explained that accountability journalism was under threat at American newspapers, particularly local ones, as a result of a combination of falling circulation, low advertising revenue, and a tendency to produce the kind of soft news that plays well on social media.[1] Oliver explained that newspapers still produce the lion's share of hard news and investigations—the kind of journalism that really matters. "It's pretty obvious [that] without newspapers around to cite, TV news would just be Wolf Blitzer endlessly batting a ball of yarn around," he explained, referring to the Cable News Network anchor. "The media is a food chain which would fall apart without local newspapers." Oliver expressed worry that newspapers would cease trying to fulfill the watchdog role in light of revenue pressure, going for "clickbait" instead of serious journalism.

To keep that from happening, Oliver begged his audience to support newspapers by paying for content, to try to keep the newspaper industry going strong. Oliver explained that keeping news organizations financially healthy allows them to pursue serious journalism, like accountability reporting. "We've just grown accustomed to getting our news for free," Oliver declared. "And the longer that we get something for free, the less willing that we are to pay for it. Sooner or later we are either going to have to pay for journalism, or we are all going to pay for it." Although Oliver was joking around, he made it clear that the issue of a strong watchdog press is no laughing matter.

And it certainly is not—particularly given the unprecedented election of 2016. The ascent of Donald Trump to the U.S. presidency requires a vibrant watchdog press more than ever before. What makes the Trump presidency particularly challenging to monitor is that he arguably has more potential areas for malfeasance, given his vast business holdings, than any previous U.S. president. "It is uncharted territory, really in the history of the republic, as we have never had a president with such an empire both in the United States and overseas," foreign policy expert Michael Green told the *New York Times*.[2] Trump's refusal to put his interests into a "blind trust" as other presidents have done has caused many Americans to worry about whether political decisions will be made to enrich his family's businesses rather than to serve the public. Not only is the president deeply involved in commerce, but so are many members of his cabinet and close advisors. "Voters have long worried about elected officials using their power to line their pockets—or those of business partners—and shape policies to advance their private interests," wrote the Associated Press. "But rarely has an incoming president represented such potential for conflicts of interest."[3] The president's tendency to lie also mandates extra vigilance from the media to fact-check his statements. Monitoring this presidential administration is tough work. It requires deep resources and global access to information—exactly the kinds of skills that newspapers bring to the task. In fact, digging out information that holds government accountable is unequivocally what papers do better than any other kind of news organization.

Yet despite the great need for the kind of watchdog reporting typically done by papers, it is hard to go a single day without reading about the decline of the newspaper industry. Americans' well-established habit of reading a daily newspaper started to fall off in the 1980s.[4] The reasons for the drop are complex but include the increasing popularity of entertainment television, sociological changes related to the suburbanization of America, and increases in newspaper prices.[5] Circulation peaked at about 63 million papers per day, a figure attained in 1984 for daily papers and in 1990 for Sunday papers.[6] After that, the circulation loss was slow and steady at first, but it accelerated because of the worldwide financial crisis of 2007.[7] During the period covered by this study, 1991–2011, American newspaper circulation declined by more than a quarter overall and by much higher amounts at some individual newspapers.[8] Most newsgathering budgets shrank as a result, as advertising revenues fell along with readership. Certainly, some newspapers have rather successfully made the transition to being multimedia news organizations and are turning a profit as a result. But many others, while providing news that is critical to their communities, are struggling to stay in the black as their readership falls, eating away the advertising base. It is no wonder that the *Financial Times* calls newspaper publishing "America's fastest-shrinking industry."[9]

The erosion of the newspaper business is very sad, but there is one reason in particular why we as citizens should be highly concerned: Day-in and day-out, no other function of a free press is as important as its ability to monitor the work of the government. As *Washington Post* editor Marty Baron put it, "[H]olding the most powerful to account is what we are *supposed* to do. If we do not do that, then what exactly *is* the purpose of journalism?"[10] Without media to act as the eyes and ears of the public, acts of government malfeasance often go unnoticed. It is easier for politicians to get away with abusing power, wasting public funds, and making poor decisions if the press is not shining its light with what is termed "accountability reporting" or "public affairs journalism." The necessity of journalists' serving as a "Fourth Estate," watching over the branches of government, remains one of our nation's core values, embodied by the First Amendment.

There can be no question whatsoever that the presence of a vibrant press to monitor government is not just important on the micro level but is essential to the proper functioning of our democracy. As media critics John Nichols and Robert McChesney put it, we are:

> [a] country that from its founding has valued the press not merely as a watchdog but as the essential nurturer of an informed citizenry. The collapse of journalism and the democratic infrastructure it sustains is not a development that anyone, except perhaps corrupt politicians and the interests they serve, looks forward to.[11]

My mentor Marvin Kalb, the Harvard professor and former television news correspondent with a long view of history, goes even further—calling a vibrant press the sturdiest bulwark against the rise of fascism and authoritarianism. "A free press guarantees a free society. That's why it's so terribly important," he says.[12] My own experience living in Russia for more than a decade bears this out; there, the erosion of meaningful democracy under President Vladimir Putin coincided with a government takeover of television news and much of the print press—and not by accident.

In fact, the work of the news media is valued because it helps empower what Jürgen Habermas termed "the public sphere," meaning "a realm of our social life in which something approaching public opinion can be formed."[13] Habermas understood the public sphere not just as a virtual or imagined place to discuss public affairs but as a mechanism to enable citizens to influence social action. He saw the news media as a critical element in that process:

> Today newspapers and magazines, radio and television are the media of the public sphere. . . . Only when the exercise of political control is effectively subordinated to the democratic demand that information be available to the public, does the political public sphere win an institutionalized influence over the government through the instrument of law-making bodies.[14]

Although the theories of the public sphere were developed decades ago, they still apply to the Internet age. Even in the age of digital communication, when politicians and bureaucrats have the ability to communicate directly with publics as never before, the news media still play an important intermediary role in helping keep governments accountable to their citizens. In fact, in this era of so-called "fake news," one could argue that newspapers and the verified facts they contain are more important to the public sphere than ever before.

This book will add to the existing literature in media studies by examining how this most important form of journalism—accountability reporting in American newspapers—has evolved in the early Internet era, focusing on the time after newspaper reading had peaked and as the Internet became widely used, 1991 to 2011. By examining the front pages of a cross-section of American newspapers, this book will provide evidence that, contrary to conventional wisdom, the newspapers studied generally held steadfast to their watchdog role during this time, despite formidable challenges. It will also delve into the question of whether newspapers are still able to dig into important stories with the kinds of long, sustained reporting efforts that are often necessary to uncover watchdog stories. The data will suggest that they do, sometimes to an unprecedented extent. The research will also suggest that this happened not only because accountability reporting lies at the very heart of what makes journalism a valued public service but because it increasingly drives many readers to pay for content. The research contained herein might not allay all of John Oliver's worries about a weakened news ecosystem, but it will suggest that American newspapers have held, not abandoned, the watchdog role, and that readers have taken notice.

The United States has a long and storied history of watchdog reporting, exemplified by the muckraking of Lincoln Steffens and his colleagues at *McClure's Magazine* at the beginning of the twentieth century and the uncovering of the Watergate scandal by Bob Woodward and Carl Bernstein of the *Washington Post* in the 1970s. Even the very first newspaper printed in the American colonies, *Publick Occurrences, Both Forreign and Domestick*, was ordered shut after just one issue in 1690 for its uncensored comments about the British government.[15] Of course, watchdog reporting today is not gone. But despite its noble history, there can be no doubt that the creation of the kind of watchdog reporting that has always existed in our nation as a counterbalance to government power faces serious obstacles in the twenty-first century.

Some of the obstacles are economic. Media organizations are under more financial pressure than ever before, as revenues drop across the industry. To cope, mainstream news organizations have shed staff and cut budgets, meaning they have fewer workers to produce content. Critics like Dean Starkman argue that this has created reporters who turn and turn like caged hamsters running on a wheel, producing lots of short and often surface stories instead of high-quality reporting. "The Hamster Wheel, then, is investigations you will never see, good work left undone, public service not performed," he writes.[16] For many news outlets, the drop in staff and the need for the remaining reporters to do more with less means they have chosen not to pursue some watchdog reporting projects, which can be relatively expensive and time-consuming to produce. "When faced with cuts, investigative reporting is often the first target," writes investigative journalist and editor Laura Frank. "Investigative journalism takes more time and more experienced journalists to produce, and it often involves legal battles. It's generally the most expensive work the news media undertakes."[17] The data described in this book will leave little doubt that some papers have been limited by their weakening economics, cutting back on both the number of accountability articles they produce overall and also the complexity of the reporting being done. But it will also show that the newspapers studied generally showed great resilience against economic pressures, mostly as a result of the commitment of their editors and publishers to the watchdog role.

Yet part of the challenge goes beyond economic pressures into issues of consumption. Audience tastes are changing, and people are increasingly turning away from news in general[18] and from lengthy reports in particu-lar.[19] In fact, the American press has become overall more shallow during the past twenty years, meaning that articles and television news reports have gotten shorter overall,[20] with shorter quotes,[21] with less serious subject matter overall.[22] This faster, tighter approach to news undoubtedly equates to less watchdog journalism, which can be longwinded and complicated. Also, the rise of opinionated cable news networks has changed the flavor of government criticism into one that is more partisan and less based on facts than before.[23] As the great political scientist James Q. Wilson put it:

> As one journalist has remarked about the change in his profession, "We don't deal in facts [any longer], but in attributed opinions." Or, these days, in unattributed opinions. And those opinions are more intensely rivalrous than was once the case. . . . Once the media talked to us; now they shout at us.[24]

This trend, too, is leading to less watchdog reporting, as some news out-lets, particularly cable news channels, have become more focused on bat-ting around opinions than on diving into deep pools of facts. And the rise of so-called "fake news" has also raised questions about whether readers want to be informed by the news or simply titillated. The trends here would seem to be depressing, rather than encouraging, the production of deep dive reporting.

Furthermore, part of the issue is technological. The Internet has drasti-cally transformed the practice of journalism, as well as everyday life. It has vastly changed the gathering and spreading of information. Many of the changes brought about in the age of digital journalism are clearly positive. Reporters say they find it easier to find sources thanks to the Internet, and most enjoy the increased contact with their audience that the web fosters. Consumers enjoy many more sources of news and now find it easier to receive information from distant places. Social media sites like Facebook and Twitter now play a huge role in delivering content to consumers and newsgathering. And the rise of smartphones as news-delivery devices has also dramatically affected consumption and dissemination of information.

While technology is making it easier to undertake accountability report-ing, there are also downsides that affect the production of public service journalism. Finding a long-term financial model for commercial journal-ism in the Internet era has proven difficult, as many consumers have been reluctant to pay for content they can receive for free on the web. Moreover, the Internet can make it difficult to determine what is true and what is false, and to separate fact from opinion. Although there was an epidemic of fake news during the election of 2016 that helped push Trump over the top, the problem of false information circulating on the Internet goes back to the rise of the World Wide Web itself. Some neuroscientists even suggest that the way information is presented on the Internet is having a bad effect on human brains, making it more difficult for people to focus.[25] The increasing audience for news being delivered on smartphones and tablets also poses special challenges for long-form reporting, like deep accountability journalism. It is somewhat inconvenient to read articles that stretch over many, many screens—even if the reader is interested in the content. The fact that economics were changing over the same time period when digital change was happening makes it complicated to attribute the effects of each, but it is clear that economics, culture, and technology have all combined to create a challenging environment for public affairs reporting.

CLUES FROM FRONT-PAGE CONTENT

A number of media critics have studied the dynamics of today's media ecosystem and concluded that the amount of journalism that monitors the work of government must have been going down overall over the past decade or two. "Much of local and state government, whole federal departments and agencies, American activities around the world, the world itself—vast areas of great public concern—are either neglected or on the verge of neglect," write Nichols and McChesney.[26] "The genre is on life-support compared to what it once was," concludes *Broadcasting & Cable*.[27] "The watchdogs have abandoned their posts," says *American Journalism Review*.[28] The view that the watchdogs have lost their bite seems to be widespread among journalists and scholars today. And several different kinds of academic studies have hit upon the challenges facing watchdog reporting, including ethnographies of newspaper production[29] and studies of the economics and technology of news.[30]

Although much work has been done already on the nature of the crisis facing American newspapers and the challenges to long-form, investigative reporting, no one has yet done a content analysis that reaches across multiple newspapers over a long period to assess the trends in the production of watchdog reporting. This book aims to remedy that situation by creating a longitudinal portrait of accountability reporting done by a varied group of American newspapers over twenty years. After all, the pages of America's newspapers really provide the clearest indication of how accountability reporting has been evolving in the digital era. For the purposes of this study, I will define "accountability reporting" as "original nonbreaking news reporting about the work of government and of public policy issues." The book will focus in particular on one of accountability reporting's subsets, watchdog reporting, wherein journalists search for malfeasance by the government through deep and sustained reporting and hold public officials accountable for their actions. This book tries to extrapolate larger trends about public service journalism by examining thousands of news stories over time.

When I first conceived of this project, I was certain that the results would be bad—even distressing. I thought I would be chronicling the death of watchdog reporting, based on my own experience as a journalist and the many discussions I have had with colleagues over the years. I had started my career as a newspaper reporter, cutting my teeth at the *Columbia Daily Spectator* and the *New York Times* in college, before working for the *Los Angeles Times* after graduate school. Although I later moved into television, spending nine years as a producer and reporter for CBS News, I maintained many friends at newspapers. It was discussions with some of them that spurred this book. One friend lamented that if the Watergate scandal happened today rather than back in 1972, few newspapers would be able to dedicate several reporters to an investigation as they had then. Others agreed that today's tight-budgeted, scaled-down newspapers might miss the Watergate story entirely, changing the course of history. That got me wondering if watchdog reporting was still vibrant. Are American newspapers still able to dedicate resources to dig out the important stories that need a sustained effort to produce? That led to me to sample the front pages of a group of American newspapers, spread across the country, of varying sizes and ownership structures, for answers.

But the content analysis came out differently from what I had imagined it would be. The data actually suggests that not only have newspapers maintained their role as watchdogs in the digital era, but also that many papers are concentrating on that role more than ever before. Because the data surprised me, I approached editors of the newspapers studied to help me understand the discrepancy between what I expected to find and what the results actually showed. Why, I asked, was there not a precipitous decline in watchdog reporting as the financial crisis at newspapers began to bite? Why did most of the newspapers I studied increase, rather than decrease, the amount of digging they did into government affairs as their budgets tightened and staff size fell? Those interviews made it clear why newspapers were not abandoning the watchdog role.

"WORK THAT MATTERS"

The editors interviewed say that first and foremost, they go out of their way to direct their limited resources into the production of public affairs journalism because it serves their newspapers' core mission. I see this *cultural* factor—that reporters and editors believe watchdog reporting is central to their purpose—as the single most important reason why newspapers continue to dedicate so many resources to their accountability reporting. Readers simply depend on newspapers to be the main investigative force in their cities. "People want us to do this. They don't think anyone else will if we don't," explains editor Kevin Riley of the *Atlanta Journal-Constitution*. "A lot of our consumers know that newspapers are under duress now, and they don't want to have a community without a newspaper."[31] I was particularly surprised to see that several of the newspapers studied here have boosted their production of public affairs journalism—even after significant staff cuts—by making a conscious effort to do so. "The truth is, it's gotten tighter for pretty much everyone. No one has the resources they had 10 years ago," explains Duchesne Drew, who was a reporter for or managing editor of the *Star Tribune* in Minneapolis during much of the study period. "We've become increasingly focused on doing work that matters."[32] Even the managing editor of the smallest paper studied for this book, the *Lewiston* (Idaho) *Tribune*, said he spends considerable resources on fulfilling the watchdog role. "We trust our reporters to actually cover their beats and come back and tell us what's going on and why it's important," explains Doug Bauer of the *Tribune*. "And if they come back and say, 'Hey, this is a huge issue I need to get to,' we're going to do everything we can to give them the time that they need to make that happen."[33] The data will demonstrate that despite drops in staffing and budget, the papers studied here value accountability stories so highly that they keep them coming, even though they can be expensive and complicated to produce.

I became particularly interested in understanding whether cultural factors, technological ones, or others were responsible for an uptick in the production of deep watchdog stories starting with the 2001 sample. Of the nine newspapers I studied, seven had more front-page accountability reporting in their 2001 samples than in 1996. And only one newspaper studied had its peak level of front-page watchdog journalism before the 2001 sample. These trend lines in the statistics suggested some factor was coming into play after the 1996 sample that was driving up accountability reporting in future years.

Although technological factors like the rise of the Internet are likely to account for some of the increase, as do economic ones like the ever-increasing pressure to turn a profit, I believe that there was also a powerful cultural response for more and better accountability journalism resulting from the most highly covered political event of the era: the scandal involving

President Bill Clinton and Monica Lewinsky, which went public in 1998. This was the first major political scandal to play out in the presence of new media and politicized cable news. (The Internet became a household item only in the latter part of the 1990s;[34] Fox News Channel and MSNBC launched in 1996.[35]) Broken on the Internet, the Clinton–Lewinsky scandal played out in round-the-clock coverage that has been described as "all-Monica, all the time."[36] There are reasons to believe that Clinton–Lewinsky actually prompted the production of accountability reporting in its aftermath, at least at American newspapers, much as Watergate had more than two decades earlier.

As they joined television as part of the "feeding frenzy"[37] of coverage, many newspapers broke some of the longstanding cultural traditions that dictate how news should be covered. For instance, a review of Marvin Kalb's book on the coverage of Clinton–Lewinsky points out that:

> The original *Washington Post* story quoted 24 anonymous sources. Gone was the *Post*'s "two-source" requirement that it imposed on itself in the Watergate era. Now one source, however flimsy, was okay. Kalb gives dozens of examples to show that the rest of the press was just as sloppy.[38]

As it became clear that the Clinton–Lewinsky story was quite serious—meaning that it was not simply a sexual scandal but one that involved possible criminal behavior, ultimately resulting in President Clinton's impeachment—newspaper reporters and editors were no doubt increasingly reminded of their obligation to produce verified, sober accountability reporting rather than the kind of breathless coverage that was dominating television. As one retired *Washington Post* correspondent complained at the time:

> Some of us trying to catch public attention from the rear of the over-sexed, over-loud, and short-on-manners media supermarket are motivated, instead, by the First Amendment's underlying purpose: To reinforce democracy in its loftiest aspirations, by giving the public the information it must have to prevent the abuse of power. That is what "watchdog" really means.[39]

I am not sure newspaper personnel became remorseful over the way they had bent some of their usual rules covering the story, particularly early on, or if the Clinton saga energized them over time and inspired them to continue to dig into the conduct of their elected officials. It is possible that both of these reactions happened. Both strike me as possible explanations for the increases in watchdog reporting picked up by my research in the sample following Clinton's impeachment. By this same line of reasoning, it seems logical to believe that the presidential election of 2000 also may have also helped encourage newspapers to rebound into accountability reporting, because of the extraordinary circumstances that led to the election of George W. Bush and the numerous issues left open to investigation in its aftermath. But I see Clinton–Lewinsky as a larger driver of change at newspapers because it happened earlier, dragged on far longer, and has been acknowledged to have completely changed the way politics is reported in America.[40]

It is important to contextualize this discussion in the larger research about how journalism changed during the Internet era, when the technological changes to journalism created cultural changes in response. The period of the mid-1990s is generally accepted to be that in which the traditional system of mainstream media as gatekeeper began to break down.[41] It was during this time that the Internet created a plethora of new outlets for reporting that did not subscribe to all the previously held norms and values of journalistic production, among them bloggers like Matt Drudge and opinionated cable news networks. Newspaper editors of the time may well have explicitly or subconsciously chosen to increase their papers' output of accountability journalism in an attempt to reassert their gatekeeping role. The rebirth of watchdog journalism at newspapers seen in the twenty-first century may also have been affected by considerable boosts in readership during and after the Clinton–Lewinsky scandal, resulting from an increased hunger for news.[42] This could also have tipped off editors and publishers that fulfilling the watchdog role could be economically as well as culturally advantageous.

REASONS TO BUY A NEWSPAPER

In fact, the second-strongest reason by my estimation for the emphasis on watchdog reporting seen throughout the study is *economic*. Editors and publishers have come to embrace the realization that strong public affairs journalism ultimately holds the key to newspapers' continued survival in a hypercompetitive and crowded field. This reflects a strategic choice to stake the papers' long-term survival on the one thing that newspapers do better than anyone else—watchdog journalism. The reason that television and magazines are not included in this work is that my preliminary research suggested that they were just not major producers of deep accountability journalism during this time;[43] it is newspapers that still carry that load. "With declining resources, newspapers like ours are doubling down on journalism that matters and has impact," says Greg Moore, former editor of *The Denver Post*, one of the papers studied. "We are letting go of the lighter fare and focusing on harder hitting reporting."[44] The results here will suggest that this focus on high-visibility accountability reporting isn't a short-term strategy but a key part of a new model for newspapers' long-term economic success.

That strategy makes watchdog journalism a way to convince readers that newspapers are worth not just *reading*, but also *buying*. "Accountability journalism is crucial to a news outlet's mission," wrote Rem Rider, once editor of the now-defunct *American Journalism Review* (*AJR*). "And it's a good strategy as well. In a world full of commodity news, it is something that makes you stand out. It can enhance your role in the community significantly. It can be your franchise."[45] And many of the editors interviewed said that readers responded very positively when they did make public affairs reporting a priority. "When we do major investigative pieces we frequently get notes from readers saying this is why they continue to support the newspaper," says Moore. "People want public service journalism and they realize it costs money to do that kind of deep reporting."[46] Editors say that in the Internet era, it is the quality of the journalism that newspapers can offer that ultimately induces many readers to pay for content that they might be able to access, at least in part, for free. "What can separate great journalism from everything else that's available is simply our commitment to the journalism of verification and to watchdog reporting," says Rex Smith, editor of the *Albany Times Union*. "It will give people a reason to seek us out. It will give us credibility that other organizations don't have, and it is really a fundamental element of sustaining the brand."[47] It is not hard to see that this strategy of success through quality is in many ways the very opposite of what some other news organizations are doing, which is to drive readership through clickbait—articles that arouse reader interest but usually offer little real substance.

The results of this study will highlight the work of papers like the *Times Union* and the *Atlanta Journal-Constitution* that have made accountability reporting a central part of their output and attracted readers in the process. This is not to say that every newspaper here has seen circulation increase as it has reemphasized accountability reporting. Several have not, while others have. Literature that examines the media through a business perspective explains that newspapers seek ways to make sound financial decisions despite tight resources. As James T. Hamilton's outstanding book on the financial benefits created for society by investigative reporting explains, "Editors operate in a world of multiple scarcities: limited audience attention, constrained staff levels, and sometimes-meager financial returns. The decision to dig deep is making a bet on whether a story will be there and the effort will pay off."[48] One of the few arguments that newspaper editors have left to induce readers to pay for content is that their papers are serving the community through watchdog journalism, and that this work is worthy of financial support.

YET MORE REASONS FOR THE WATCHDOGS TO BARK

Another important part of the rise of watchdog reporting identified by my research is the *technological* factor: the rise of the Internet, which enhanced and enabled the kind of information gathering that is needed to do deep dive reporting. The advent of the Internet made it easier to find people and contact them via e-mail, access government databases, file Freedom of Information Act requests, and use complex computer-assisted reporting technologies. Later on, social media opened up even more new avenues to collect and spread information for stories, as social media, including Twitter and Facebook, gained popularity. The digital environment also created all kinds of opportunities for journalists to harness readers as contributors to accountability reporting, thereby increasing reader engagement. Editors interviewed for this book say that accountability stories typically do not do as well digitally as lighter fare, but they still can garner good metrics. Watchdog stories are often given high visibility by sites that do news aggregation like Google News or the Daily Beast, which also spurs additional readership. Even when the person clicking on a post doesn't read the entire article, which is the norm these days,[49] the sharing and aggregation create clicks, driving up the bottom line of the newspapers creating the content.

The influence of the Internet on the production of journalism is so significant that it must have contributed to the rise in watchdog output revealed by this research. But I have concluded that it is not quite as important as the cultural and financial factors because the promise of the Internet was not always reflected in the data I collected. For instance, I expected to see the number of sources used per article go up after the advent of the Internet, because it is so easy to find and contact people for interviews in a wired world. But that was not borne out by the data. The average number of sources quoted in the stories coded in the 1991 sample was 5.79 and was almost unchanged in the 2011 sample at 5.81. Similarly, average story length started and ended the study period at about the same level, near 1,275 words.[50] I had theorized that the story length might have increased as the Internet made it easier to gather and publish information. Furthermore, fewer stories in 2011 quoted publicly available documents than in 1991, which was quite surprising given the ease with which documents can be found through online searches.[51] The overall mix of sources among categories like government officials, businesspeople, experts, or affected individuals also changed very little over the study period, despite its becoming increasingly easy to find potential sources on the Internet. I had hoped that a more diverse group of sources might have appeared thanks to online resources, but this was not indicated by the data. Newspapers became more, not less, reliant on government sources over time, worryingly so at the smallest papers.[52] And investigations became less complex generally over the length of the study, moving away from examinations of large processes or enterprises and toward wrongdoing by a single person.[53] This is somewhat worrisome, as it suggests that gains made in the ability to dig by the Internet were offset by losses in personnel and funding.

Another reason for the rise in watchdog reporting noted by this study is *professional*: that this kind of reporting is likely to win prizes, thereby boosting prestige. Editors told me they don't do public service journalism just to win prizes, but awards do raise a newspaper's reputation and profile. So many editors mentioned the quest for prizes that it seems a very real reason for their encouraging the production of deep dive reporting on government, policy, and business—though this strikes me as less important than the other reasons I have already discussed. Prizes must be a relatively small part of the calculus that goes on in editors' minds, as no one can ever be sure of winning a prestigious journalism prize. The competition for top awards is just too fierce. Besides, journalism prizes have already been around and inspiring reporters for a long time.

The fact that many papers studied for this book demonstrated similar growth in their accountability reporting even though they have vastly different cultures, finances, circulations, locations, and ownership structures suggests that the expansion of watchdog reporting despite the challenges is no fluke, nor are their editors "tooting their own horns" when it comes to what they do. Rather, it suggests a new and widely adopted strategy for the survival of the American newspaper—to provide the critical deep dive reporting that no other kind of organization can match, fulfilling a crucial and highly valued need in the community, taking advantage of the technological improvements to journalism, adding to the profession's overall excellence.[54] The experiences of the nine newspapers covered by the study suggest that as much as news content may entertain, its value as a unique source of reporting that fulfills the all-important watchdog role may be the key to the industry's staying afloat in today's choppy waters. It turns out that readers like the sound of media watchdogs barking loudly.

When I first came up with the idea for this examination of different newspaper cohorts and their approaches to their watchdog role, I assumed that I would be able to piggyback onto existing content analyses of accountability journalism, updating them for the current landscape and bringing them into the Internet era. This proved to be difficult, because there were very few studies of accountability journalism centered on content analysis on which to base my research. While there are already plenty of books about how to *do* investigative reporting, I failed to find a single academic study done in the past two decades that focused on American investigative reporting on a national level using content analysis, and only a handful of studies that addressed aspects of investigative reporting on the local level.[55] And not a single study addressed watchdog reporting (as opposed to general investigative reporting) in any broad, systematic way that involved large-scale content analysis. There are such studies in English about the accountability work of the foreign press, including excellent books on the watchdog press in South America[56] and China,[57] but I did not find their equivalents in the United States. This particular gap in our understanding of journalism studies is both good and bad; while it was difficult to have so little preexisting research on which to base my work, the dearth of literature suggested that this topic has been understudied so far.

To answer all these questions about the changing nature of accountability reporting, I collected and then analyzed data across a broad sample of newspapers to determine precisely how watchdog and investigative reporting have changed over the past twenty years, as the Internet has come of age and media organizations have fallen under extreme financial pressures. The data collection was aimed at determining the extent to which newspapers have done reporting that digs deep to reveal hidden information, fulfilling the watchdog function of the American press. The book also examines how these news organizations chose to use their limited resources and how their choices evolved as the Internet spread and flourished. To that end, this research sidesteps breaking news, which I argue news organizations *must* cover, to focus on the original stories relating to government and public policy that newspapers *choose* to cover with their remaining resources. This is an important point, central to understanding the content analysis; this examination has excluded breaking news coverage in order to focus on what is generally called "enterprise journalism," the original reports that reporters and their editors generate though thought and brainstorming. "Enterprise stories go beyond the ones that reporters would naturally cover—a routine beat story, breaking news or a planned event," explains one journalism guidebook. "Developing enterprise stories can be a challenge because it takes patience and perseverance to be creative."[58] In particular, this project examines how much of the original enterprise reporting on government and policy in the samples studied actually *digs deep* into issues rather than just skims the surface. To put it another way, this study's aim is to differentiate when the press chooses to use its scant resources to pick the "low-hanging fruit" and when it invests time and effort to climb to the "tops of the trees."

Although I originally collected data from different kinds of media, there was reason going in to believe that newspapers were the medium most worthy of study. "Despite all the development of other media, the fact is that newspapers in recent years have continued to field the majority of reporters and to produce most of the original news stories in cities across the country," Paul Starr has observed.[59] The existing evidence suggests that newspapers are the main engine that drives investigative reporting in the American media. One study that showed this was a 2011 investigation of the news environment of Baltimore, done by the Pew Research Center's Project for Excellence in Journalism.[60] That study analyzed all sources of news reporting in Baltimore during one week—including newspapers, television, talk radio, and news blogs—to ascertain which organizations actually created original content versus which repeated news that others had reported. The authors found that although there were more news outlets than ever, many of them were little more than echo chambers, repeating news that had been broken by others—mainly by newspapers:

> Among the six major news threads studied in depth—which included stories about budgets, crime, a plan involving transit buses, and the sale of a local theater—fully 83% of stories were essentially repetitive, conveying no new information. Of the 17% that did contain new information, nearly all [of it] came from traditional media either in their legacy platforms or in new digital ones.[61]

The study found that general and niche newspapers accounted for 61 percent of the total amount of enterprise reporting done during that one-week study period, with television news and its websites providing 28 percent. And Internet-only news sites and other "new media" in that study did almost no enterprise reporting, with just 4 percent of their stories containing original information. The newspapers and television stations that provided the bulk of news in this study were, not surprisingly, the largest and most financially robust news organizations in Baltimore.

Additional analyses like the one done by Nate Silver, then a reporter and statistician for the *New York Times*, provide additional evidence that newspapers do the lion's share of original reporting.[62] Silver searched Google News and Google Blogs for references to news reported by specific news organizations—for example, that "the *New York Times* reported" something—over one month in 2011. He was trying to measure the number of times that a news organization broke a piece of news that was so important or original that other news organizations would re-report it. This effort did not capture every reference to pieces of original reporting, but it did suggest patterns of news production. After doing this for a very large array of news organizations, Silver came up with a snapshot of who creates news. Silver found that thirteen of the top twenty-five news producers in his study were newspapers. He also identified the one hundred top producers of original reporting, of which sixty-five were newspapers. This, too, suggests that in the current media environment, newspapers are still the dominant creators of enterprise reporting.

The dominance of newspapers as a creator of accountability journalism was also confirmed by my own data collection. After examining the output of one network evening news show (*NBC Nightly News*) and three magazines (*The New Yorker*, *Time*, and *The Atlantic*) over a twenty-year horizon with the help of my research assistants, I concluded that the sampled television and magazine media produced very little deep watchdog or investigative reporting. They did lots of enterprise reporting, but very little of it was deep in nature or aimed at ferreting out malfeasance by either government or private industry. After several months of research into magazines and television, I decided to focus this book on newspapers, which still produce high quantities of accountability reporting.

To do so, I collected and then analyzed data about the coverage of government and public policy issues in a wide sample of American newspapers. This data collection and content analysis was aimed at discovering the kinds of reporting techniques being used today and the reporting choices being made to cover stories on government operations and public policy issues.

ORGANIZATIONS STUDIED

I gathered data for a sample of nine newspapers, stratified into three groups to allow for comparisons based on size and scope. The newspapers were specifically chosen to represent wide geographical diversity, to ensure that there was no area-specific bias to the results. The nine papers were also chosen to reflect a wide range of corporate and private ownership structures—independent, small chains, and diversified media companies. In addition, all the papers studied needed to be available in electronic form going back to the start of the study period: April 1, 1991. This was not an issue in terms of choosing large or medium-sized newspapers, but there were not many small newspapers available in electronic form going back to 1991. Using the resources of Fordham University, where I teach, and the NewsLibrary archival site (nl.newsbank.com), I was able to come up with three small newspapers to study, located in different parts of the United States, with differing ownership structures. Of course, these nine newspapers only suggest, not prove, the underlying trends in the newspaper business. However, this wide range of papers was specifically chosen to create a portrait that would shed light on the larger newspaper industry in America.

The first cohort, to be discussed at length in Chapter 2, consisted of three large national newspapers, which I will refer to as the "Large Newspaper Group":

- *New York Times*
- *Wall Street Journal*
- *Washington Post*

These three papers can be considered to be national leaders in reporting, with large staffs and considerable resources. My hypothesis was that these papers have done and still do large amounts of original reporting and relatively large amounts of watchdog reporting, although I theorized that these newspapers had likely all cut back on the amount of deep accountability reporting they produced over time as a result of limits on resources. Of all of these papers, my theory was that the *Washington Post*, as the newspaper of the nation's capital, should do the most watchdog reporting, particularly about the federal government, of the three. I expected to find the *New York Times* a close second in overall quantity, a hypothesis that did not turn out to be correct. Another hypothesis was that the *Wall Street Journal*, because of its strong business orientation, would do the most investigative reporting related to business, particularly with regard to business–government relations. These kinds of investigations of private businesses were relevant to this study when they involved public policy issues.

The second group of papers studied was medium-sized newspapers, which I will refer to as the "Metropolitan Dailies." This group started with three papers:

- *Atlanta Journal-Constitution*
- *Minneapolis Star Tribune*
- *Denver Post*

I ended up adding a fourth paper to this group:

- *Albany* (New York) *Times Union*

The *Times Union* had originally been included with the small newspaper group but was moved because it was so large that it acted more like a medium-sized paper than a small one. Those in the original group of three—the Atlanta, Minneapolis, and Denver papers—are all relatively close in circulation and located in cities that are relatively similar in size. Moreover, Atlanta, Denver, and Minneapolis can all be considered regional capitals—cities that fuel the economic growth of their regions, which might not be said of Albany.

I went into this study unsure of precisely how committed these metropolitan dailies were to their watchdog role, given how gravely they were affected by the economic turndown that began in 2007. Given the prevailing conventional wisdom about the cuts to watchdog journalism, my hypothesis was that the medium-sized newspapers had cut back on their deep accountability reporting. This turned out to be far from the case, as all four papers had deep commitments to watchdog journalism. The results of this part of the content analysis are presented in Chapter 3.

The third group studied was local newspapers, which I will refer to as the "Small Newspaper Group." This group started with three papers, but after I removed the *Albany Times Union*, two papers remained:

- *Bradenton* (Florida) *Herald*
- *Lewiston* (Idaho) *Tribune*

My theory was that the smallest newspapers probably did not have the resources at any point over the twenty-year horizon of this study to do much watchdog reporting, and that any ability they did have to do deep accountability journalism might have been adversely affected by the 2007 financial crisis. This turned out to be partially true. The *Bradenton Herald* did deep accountability reporting at a low yet steady level, even as its financial position became stretched thinner over time. But the smallest paper in my study, the *Lewiston Tribune*, did almost no deep reporting at all during the five study years surveyed. I also theorized that the smaller the paper, the more trouble it would have in dedicating resources to deep accountability reporting, which was supported by the data. These results for the two small newspapers, the *Bradenton Herald* and *Lewiston Tribune*, will be detailed in Chapter 4. In the end, I ended up considering three large papers, four medium-sized papers, and two small papers in stratified groups.

STORY CLASSIFICATIONS

A central part of the content analysis involved choosing stories for analysis that could be considered enterprise stories focusing on public policy. The content analysis also required identifying stories that involved deep reporting techniques. To do this, for all nine newspapers studied, I started my research by examining the front-page coverage in one randomly selected month, April, in five years, spaced out to be five years apart. I chose this month using a random-number generator, and it was fortunate that my selection was not November or December, when there might be an over-estimation of the number of watchdog stories because of the fact that during those months, papers are trying to publish more big articles in time for awards consideration.[63] This meant that for the newspapers, I examined every front-page story for the entire month of April in 1991, 1996, 2001, 2006, and 2011 to produce a longitudinal portrait of news coverage.

Why only the front page? First of all and most of all, I did not have the resources to examine every story on a given day during my study period. I had to limit my analysis in a way that made it possible to complete it in a reasonable amount of time. Moreover, it is well established in both the newspaper business and in the academic study of journalism that the front page is a reflection of newspapers' character and priorities. As a study of the changing American newspapers explains, "The front page not only reflects the economic climate of the newspaper industry, it mirrors the editorial instincts of newspaper ownership and staff and also attempts to meet the needs and desires of readers and ultimately society."[64] Thousands of academic studies over the decades have examined newspapers' front pages, no doubt because they provide a straightforward vehicle by which to assess content and study comparisons.

Given my experience as a newspaper reporter and my interviews with the editors of the publications studied here, my belief was that the majority of serious watchdog or investigative reports would appear on the newspapers' front pages. After all, standard operating procedure at pretty much every newspaper on Earth is to put the most important stories on the front page rather than inside. "If we had an exclusive or important what you call deep dive reporting story, of course we want to play it strongly," explains

Joseph Lelyveld, who served as the *New York Times'* top editor from 1994 to 2001.[65] Because of this, I believe the front page to be a good indicator of the overall quality for the newspapers studied, and the likely place for in-depth reports about the work of government and business to be placed. I acknowledge that this analysis does not nearly capture all the deep accountability reporting being done by the papers studied. "We generally run only two or three stories on our front page," says Moore of *The Denver Post*. "We use our other section fronts to display serious enterprise report-ing efforts. You can find solid journalism in *The Post* on almost any page."[66] Still, the front page can be used as a device to assess how content has evolved over time. After all, this study is suggesting, rather than proving, what has happened over twenty years in newspaper coverage. But I believe the conclusions I draw here are well supported because the data collected and interview material gathered show consistent trends.

I then had to determine which stories to examine in depth as examples of accountability reporting. I personally read every story in the twenty-year sample in all nine newspapers and eliminated those that consisted of breaking news. My reasoning is that when news happens, newspapers are obligated to cover it. Moreover, the focus of this study is what newspapers choose to cover with their limited resources, so I also eliminated stories that had no relation whatsoever to public policy or politics—including pure features, sports, entertainment, and business stories with no relation to policy issues. This left the stories about government and policy that each news organization *chose* to do with its limited resources. These remaining enterprise stories are what I termed the study's "accountability journalism" or "public affairs reporting," and where I focused my efforts. In all, 5,571 newspaper stories that appeared on the front pages of the nine newspapers studied were examined. Of these, 1,491 of the newspaper stories were cho-sen to be examined in depth as part of the content analysis because they were examples of enterprise journalism involving issues of public policy.

I then broke the accountability stories into two categories to differenti-ate which were simple to complete and which took actual digging. This determined which reports were classified as "simple enterprise" stories that took a few hours or days to complete, relying on interviews and straight-forward reporting techniques like a review of published documents, and which were the kinds of accountability reporting that dug into a story over weeks or months to ferret out information that would have remained secret without the journalists' work—termed here "deep accountability."

The first category, "simple enterprise" encompasses the vast majority of articles included in this study. A "simple enterprise" story involves simple reporting techniques and has no sustained digging:

- "Simple enterprise" stories are original to the newspaper, and deal with government action, government officials, or public policy issues but are not truly investigative or watchdog in nature, nor are they breaking news.
- These stories tend to be reported through interviews, direct observation, and already published documents like government reports or previous news articles.
- These stories take a day or just a few days to report.
- These stories do not involve substantive archival research or public information requests.

What I call "simple enterprise" stories inform the public about the work of government, and as such they form knowledge that helps create accountability, even if the articles do not involve deep reporting or scrutiny. However, they do not usually uncover information that is not easily accessible. An example of this kind of story can be found in the April 30, 1996, *Atlanta Journal-Constitution* story "Rite of Spring: Tag deadline brings long lines,"[67] which described lines up to two hours long to renew car registrations at Georgia Department of Motor Vehicles offices. The report involved interviews and observation, and though it elucidated the work of their government for readers, the reporting did not require real digging.

The second category involves deep reporting:

- "Deep accountability" stories are in-depth stories that investigate and evaluate the work of the government, usually using advanced reporting techniques. In general, to be considered a true watchdog story, articles had to go the extra mile to expose information that would have been hidden from the public without the journalist's efforts.
- This study uses a definition of watchdog reporting from scholars W. Lance Bennett and William Serrin: "(1) independent scrutiny by the press of the activities of government, business and other public institutions, with an aim toward (2) documenting, questioning, and investigating those activities, in order to (3) provide publics and officials with timely information on issues of public concern."[68]
- These stories involve digging. They often involve reporting methods beyond interviews, including document analysis, leaks, and Freedom of Information Act requests.
- These stories may take several weeks or even months to report.
- Deep accountability stories may concern the work of governmental, quasi-governmental, or nongovernmental actors but always have a link to public policy.

A good example of what is meant by deep accountability reporting by this study's standards is an April 10, 2011, report in the *Minneapolis Star Tribune*, entitled "State ignores teacher licensing violations."[69] The reporters for this story requested, obtained, and then analyzed state education department records to reveal that more than 900 teachers had been at work without the proper licenses during the previous five years. The work of the reporters brought to light information that likely would have stayed hidden without their sustained efforts. This is a classic example of what I mean by "deep accountability" reporting because the journalists went the extra mile to uncover the story, performing the watchdog role.

But such stories need not be about governmental actors to be considered accountability journalism. A good example of an investigation of a corporation that involves public policy issues and so would fall into this study's "deep accountability" category is a 2001 *Wall Street Journal* article entitled "Seeds of Doubt: Some Ingredients Are Genetically Modified, Despite Labels' Claims."[70] For this story, the *Journal* funded independent laboratory testing which proved that many foods that companies claimed were free of genetically modified content actually did have GMOs. That extra step of undertaking lab testing to investigate the claims of the private companies is what took that article from being a "simple enterprise" story into the realm of "deep accountability." The lab testing provided scrutiny. And although the focus of the story was corporations rather than the government, it was classified as "deep accountability" because of its focus on public health issues.

DATA GATHERED

Once I decided which articles were to be coded and how they were to be classified, my student researchers and I then created the basis for a more detailed analysis by deciding to collect information about more than twenty different aspects of each story. Among the data gathered were topic, main actors, geographic focus, types of reporting techniques used, and categories of people interviewed. Other metrics included story length, topics, and sourcing. Most of the stories were coded by a student researcher first and then checked by me. I alone coded about 10 percent of the stories. Because I checked or did all the coding, there should be no issues here about inter-coder reliability.

Often, I will compare the "pre-Internet" results with the "post-Internet" results. By "pre-Internet," I mean before the Internet became widely used in the late 1990s. This figure encompasses the 1991 and 1996 samples. The "post-Internet" figures are those from after the World Wide Web became a factor in everyday life in the United States, meaning the 2001, 2006, and 2011 samples. We are obviously not really "post-Internet" now, as the Internet remains an important instrument in most Americans' lives; these terms are just shorthand for before and after the Internet became widely used.

THE WATCHDOGS ARE BARKING, OFTEN LOUDLY

The study results suggest that despite popular belief, watchdog reporting is far from dead. The aggregated data from the nine newspapers shows clear and steady growth in deep accountability reporting. The data analysis also suggests that despite the financial challenges faced by newspapers, particularly since 2007, newspapers have not abandoned their watchdog role.

By comparing the total amount of deep accountability reporting in all nine newspapers studied, I found that its overall output has been going up over the past twenty years, not down. Table 1–1 shows the nine papers ranked from highest to lowest in terms of percentage of front-page content that is "deep accountability" during the five months sampled between 1991 and 2011. The percentages of front-page stories that were deep accountability reports in the nine papers studied increased slowly but steadily over the twenty-year course of the study, from a low of 1.26 percent in the first year studied, 1991, to 4.46 percent in the last year studied, 2011.

TABLE 1-1. Deep Accountability Reports as a Percentage of Front-Page Stories, Ranked from Highest to Lowest, Nine Newspaper Study Group, Months of April, 1991–2011

Newspaper	1991	1996	2001	2006	2011	Average
Wall Street Journal	1.28%	2.33%	5.88%	5.26%	4.85%	**4.03%**
Washington Post	1.51%	3.55%	4.23%	2.72%	7.74%	**3.80%**
Albany Times Union	6.35%	1.22%	3.45%	4.12%	3.61%	**3.64%**
Denver Post	0.00%	4.85%	1.80%	3.06%	5.13%	**2.92%**
Minneapolis Star Tribune	2.46%	1.15%	1.83%	2.86%	5.00%	**2.68%**
New York Times	0.34%	0.93%	4.35%	5.43%	3.19%	**2.46%**
Atlanta Journal-Constitution	1.20%	0.00%	1.06%	1.75%1	1.84%	**2.30%**
Bradenton Herald (FL)	0.93%	1.61%	1.14%	1.27%	1.44%	**1.26%**
Lewiston Tribune (ID)	0.00%	0.00%	0.00%	0.00%	1.45%	**0.32%**
Average	1.26%	1.81%	2.92%	3.25%	4.46%	**2.69%**
Change from previous		43.81%	61.54%	14.67%	38.71%	

The winners in terms of highest percentage of deep accountability during the study period are not too surprising, as the *Wall Street Journal* and
the *Washington Post* are two of the largest papers in the United States. The
Journal had the highest percentage of deep accountability overall, at 4.03
percent of all front-page stories sampled, and the *Post* was second at 3.8
percent of front-page stories. But the third paper on the list is one I would
not have predicted: the *Albany Times Union*, one of the smaller ones studied. Although the *Times Union* had the highest percentage of deep accountability reporting of the nine papers in only one of the five years studied,
1991, it nevertheless had a sustained level of deep public affairs journalism
overall, with 3.64 percent of sampled front-page stories classified as deep
accountability overall.

Looking at these same results by cohort, it is easy to see that as one
might expect, the largest and best-funded newspapers produce the lion's
share of deep dive public service journalism. The percentage of front-page
"deep accountability" reports for each newspaper group is summarized in
Table 1-2.

TABLE 1-2. Deep Accountability Reports by Newspaper Cohort as a Percentage of
Front-page Stories, Nine Newspaper Study Group, Months of April, 1991–2011

Group	1991	1996	2001	2006	2011	Average
Large Newspaper Group	0.87%	1.98%	4.55%	4.32%	5.16%	**3.21%**
Metropolitan Dailies	2.04%	1.84%	1.82%	3.14%	6.23%	**2.76%**
Small Newspaper Group	0.58%	0.69%	0.57%	0.57%	0.90%	**0.68%**
Total	1.26%	1.81%	2.92%	3.25%	4.46%	**2.69%**

It is not surprising to see that the large papers—the *Times*, the *Post*, and
the *Journal*—produced more front-page deep accountability reporting in
the study months than the other papers. But what did surprise me is that
the metropolitan dailies produced only about 15 percent fewer deep
accountability reports, which was a much stronger result than I was
expecting to see. In fact, the medium-sized papers—those in Atlanta,
Minneapolis, Denver, and Albany—produced a higher percentage of deep
accountability stories in the 2011 sample than the other papers, as they had
in the 1991 sample. This suggests that the medium-sized newspaper segment is investing more and more heavily in accountability journalism as a
way to attract and retain readers. These findings will be discussed in more
detail in Chapter 3. The examination of deep dive public service journalism suggests that while small papers have not abandoned the watchdog
role, they are not producing at the level of the larger, richer papers. The

small-newspaper segment produced about 80 percent fewer "deep account-ability" stories than the large papers over the study period, and about 75 percent fewer than the metropolitan dailies. This would seem to confirm the concerns of those people who worry that local papers lack the resources to act as vibrant watchdogs over their communities.

The data strongly suggests that newspapers studied became better able to create deep dive accountability reports in the digital era. Looking at the entire nine-newspaper cohort, 1.51 percent of front-page content consisted of "deep accountability" reporting in the two "pre-Internet" study years, 1991 and 1996. But in the three "post-Internet" study years of 2001, 2006, and 2011, the percentage of front-page "deep accountability" content jumped to more than 3.50 percent. To put that another way, the newspapers studied were able to double the percentage of deep dive accountability reports they placed in their most visible spot, the front page, after the Internet became a factor in creating and spreading reporting. While the advent of the World Wide Web was not the only factor influencing the increase in watchdog reporting after 1996, it seems logical to think that the increased capabilities of digital journalism helped counteract some of the factors conspiring against the creation of public service reporting.

Another widely accepted assertion about newspapers in the digital area that is confirmed by this research is that as the Internet has risen in popu-larity, newspapers have been freed up from breaking news coverage and able to create more enterprise stories. An examination of the amount of "simple enterprise" reporting across all nine newspapers studied showed a slow and steady rise, as detailed in Table 1-3.

TABLE 1-3. "Simple Enterprise" Reports as a Percentage of Stories Examined, Nine Newspaper Study Group, Months of April, 1991–2011

Newspaper	1991	1996	2001	2006	2011	Average
Minneapolis Star Tribune	31.97%	36.78%	22.02%	34.29%	41.00%	**32.89%**
Washington Post	25.63%	27.41%	31.92%	37.50%	36.13%	**31.43%**
Albany Times Union	47.62%	23.17%	28.74%	17.53%	36.14%	**29.37%**
Denver Post	23.33%	22.33%	28.83%	29.59%	43.59%	**28.96%**
Lewiston (ID) *Tribune*	22.22%	15.25%	40.74%	28.33%	23.19%	**25.80%**
Wall Street Journal	30.77%	22.09%	23.53%	22.11%	27.18%	**25.06%**
Bradenton (FL) *Herald*	19.44%	33.87%	32.95%	21.52%	19.42%	**24.16%**
Atlanta Journal-Constitution	14.97%	11.11%	13.30%	30.70%	48.68%	**20.52%**
New York Times	10.51%	9.29%	18.26%	19.57%	28.72%	**15.82%**
Average	21.52%	19.78%	24.46%	27.26%	32.59%	24.94%

The fact that the amount of "simple enterprise" as defined by this study is highest in the 2011 sample suggests that as the Internet was developing as a source of hard news, newspapers were responding by dedicating more of their resources to their own original reports. In order to judge the effect of the Internet, compare the amounts of "simple enterprise" in 1991 and 1996, before the Internet was widely available, with the amounts afterward. The amount of "simple enterprise" in the nine newspapers averaged 20.7 percent in the two pre-Internet years, versus 28.1 percent in the three post-Internet ones—a jump of more than 35 percent. This suggests a significant effect on the allocation of resources away from breaking news coverage toward newspapers' own original stories over time. This, too, provides clues into how American newspapers are coping today. They simply must create original stories—meaningful stories—rather than just repeat information easily found elsewhere.

The amount of "simple enterprise" stories seen on the front pages also suggests that the newspapers studied approach their newsgathering efforts differently. The newspaper with the largest percentage of "simple enterprise" on its front pages over the twenty-year sample is the *Minneapolis Star Tribune*, where almost 33 percent of the front pages sampled from 1991 to 2011 were original, simple-to-report stories on government and policy issues. The high percentage of original enterprise in the *Star Tribune* makes intuitive sense given the presence of a competing newspaper, the *St. Paul Pioneer Press*, in the Twin Cities. Each one of those two papers needs to create original reporting to lure readers away from the other and keep the ones it has. The newspaper with the least "simple enterprise" overall is the *New York Times*. This is not particularly surprising, given that the *Times* sees itself as a national paper of record and so dedicates much of its front-page space to breaking news and its own unique and often agenda-setting deep accountability reports.

I will now turn to discussing each segment of the newspaper industry in more detail. Chapter 2 presents the results of the study of three large national newspapers. Chapter 3 presents the results of a content analysis of four metropolitan dailies. Chapter 4 presents the result of another content analysis, this one of two small local papers. And Chapter 5 contains conclusions and prescriptions for strengthening watchdog reporting.

Bigger Means Better

Some organizations seem inexorably linked to watchdog reporting. This chapter digs into the work of three of them: the large national newspapers with high circulation and big reputations for excellence. They are the *New York Times* (*NYT* or *Times*), the *Washington Post* (*Post* or *WaPo*), and the *Wall Street Journal* (*WSJ* or *Journal*). You would expect these high-achieving, well-funded news organizations to be the largest producers of watchdog journalism. This study showed that to be true, although not quite as much as one might think. Although the large papers were the highest producers of deep accountability reporting in the study group overall, they were surprisingly low producers during the early study years. It was only after the 1996 sample that the large papers examined became vibrant watchdogs. Although their reputations were always high, a look back with hindsight shows that even the largest, strongest newspapers faced challenges in producing a steady stream of watchdog reporting during the time covered by this research.

These three papers were picked for study because they are widely considered to be the most influential ones in the United States. They are all in the national top ten in terms of total circulation and dominate not only in Pulitzers but also other journalism prize competitions as well.[1] They also all fall into the top ten original sources of news in the United States,[2] and all have prominent places in American journalism. The *Times* is widely seen as the largest and strongest news organization overall—the national "paper of record." The *Washington Post* is the dominant paper in the nation's capital. And the *Wall Street Journal* is the leading business newspaper. Research also suggests these three newspapers along with *USA Today* are tops in terms of having their content spread by Twitter.[3] These top newspapers should give an indication of best practices in terms of deep dive reporting. And they do—but to my surprise, they didn't always lead the pack.

My theory was that these national newspapers, as the largest and richest, would have the most deep investigative and watchdog reporting. After all, it seemed logical to argue that they would be most able to dedicate resources to the production of labor-intensive journalism. I was fairly sure that my research would show that these papers had the resources to be relatively large producers of deep watchdog journalism in the early years studied. "We had a very big staff," explains Joseph Lelyveld, executive editor of the *New York Times* from 1994 to 2001. "And we could just do more. And we kind of delighted in doing more."[4] But it was unclear to me upon entering the study whether these large papers had been able to maintain their deep reporting at high levels over time, or whether cuts in staff and in revenues in recent years had resulted in cutbacks in accountability reporting. After all, the three papers had all suffered from the same market forces during the study period as were hitting the entire newspaper industry. To determine the answer, I examined 2,615 front-page stories in the three newspapers—1,220 in the *New York Times*, 948 in the *Washington Post*, and 447 in the *Wall Street Journal*.

DIVING INTO DEEP DIVE REPORTING

The surprise here was that early in the study years, when the three large papers had the largest staffs and budgets, they actually produced deep accountability journalism at a *lower* rate than in the later study years— when they were smaller and leaner. Although counter-intuitive, these results suggest that these three large newspapers have become better producers of deep dive public affairs reporting over time, even as their resources have waned. *Waned* is really a relative term, because a *New York Times* or *Wall Street Journal* in its 2011, slimmed-down version still had more reporters than probably any other newspaper in the nation. And those large papers, like the entire newspaper industry, had to produce multimedia journalism in the later study years as opposed to print only in the early ones—making it all the more remarkable that their commitment to deep dive reporting on public policy issues actually expanded over time.

These large papers may not have started out as the vibrant watchdogs I expected to find, but they certainly ended up being them. The specifics are contained in Table 2–1, which shows that the total combined amount of "deep accountability reporting" in the samples of the three large papers expanded by more than five times from 1991 to 2011.

The total percentage of deep accountability stories in the papers' samples jumped from less than 1 percent of all front-page stories in 1991 to more than 5 percent in 2011. This jump was not at all what I was expecting to see—but then again, I wasn't expecting the 1991 and 1996 samples to show such small amounts of deep accountability reporting. Table 2–1 also contains the raw numbers of deep accountability reports in each of the three newspapers in each year sampled. The *Times* and *Journal* basically went from producing a deep watchdog story once a month in 1991 to several per week in 2001, 2006, and 2011. The *Post*, which produced at a higher rate in the early samples, essentially went from one deep public service piece a week up to three. This represents a vast increase in the amount of deep dive reporting being done over time by these three prominent newspapers. Of course, the sample is just a suggestion of what was happening, and it is theoretically possible that April 1991 and April 1996 were statistical anom-

TABLE 2–1. Number and Percentage of Deep Accountability Reports, Large Newspaper Group, Months of April, 1991–2011

Newspaper		1991	1996	2001	2006	2011	Totals/Avg.
New York Times	# Front-page deep accountability Stories	1	3	10	10	6	30
	% Front-page deep accountability stories	0.34%	0.93%	4.35%	5.43%	3.19%	2.46%
Wash. Post	# Front-page deep accountability stories	3	7	9	5	12	36
	% Front-page deep accountability stories	1.51%	3.55%	4.23%	2.72%	7.74%	3.80%
Wall Street Journal	# Front-page deep accountability stories	1	2	5	5	5	18
	% Front-page deep accountability stories	1.28%	2.33%	5.88%	5.26%	4.85%	4.03%
Totals	**# Front-page deep accountability stories**	5	12	24	20	23	84
	% Front-page deep accountability stories	0.87%	1.98%	4.55%	4.32%	5.16%	3.21%

alies. But the fact that the same pattern was visible in all three large newspapers suggests that the content analysis is indicative of a trend.

DIGITAL, OR MORE?

But what are we to make of the timing of the jump in production in deep public service stories? The increase in deep output at the large papers was greatest starting in the 2001 sample, when the percentage of deep accountability reporting surged at all three papers from its 1996 levels. Something changed between 1996 and 2001 that drove up deep accountability reporting at all three papers. I am not sure we will ever know exactly what caused the uptick in deep dive accountability reporting at those large papers starting sometime after 1996. But the consistency of the upswing at all three papers suggests that some common factors were driving them to dig more and to go deeper.

Beyond the rise of the Internet and the reaction to the Clinton–Lewinsky scandal, I can point to one more factor mentioned in Chapter 1 that seems like a powerful driver of accountability reporting at these large newspapers: increased appetite for journalism awards. The *New York Times*, the *Washington Post*, the *Wall Street Journal*, and the *Los Angeles Times* won so many awards beginning in the 1980s that the *Columbia Journalism Review* dubbed the four papers "the Pulitzer Cartel."[5] Those four newspapers won about one-third of the Pulitzers in the 1990s and nearly half in the decade from 2000 to 2009.[6] Although they would hardly admit it, the three national papers I studied seem to have been so driven to win prizes that they dedicated resources to precisely the kind of journalism that wins accolades—deep investigations and watchdog stories.

The five-times jump in deep accountability reporting over the length of the study period across the whole three-paper cohort suggests that despite the financial and personnel challenges, large newspapers saw and still see deep reporting as a priority. Their editors say that is because this reporting is so central to their missions. "You have to go deep and be authoritative doing what I call 'how, why, will' stories: how did something happen, why did something happen, what's going to happen next?" explains Marcus Brauchli, former top editor of both the *Washington Post* and the *Wall Street Journal*. "Those are the stories that people cannot get or generally don't look for in the course of a day."[7] This may help explain why the *Washington Post* did so much deep accountability reporting in the study period. The numbers of *Post* reports classified by this study as "deep accountability" rose from just four in the April 1991 *WP* sample to twelve in April 2011, highlighting the paper's growing commitment to serious accountability reporting.

Percentage-wise, the *Wall Street Journal* actually came in first in the total percentage of deep accountability reporting among the large national papers, and also in the entire nine-paper sample overall. The *WSJ* puts far fewer stories on its front pages than do its competitors, meaning that despite lower raw numbers of deep accountability reports, a higher percentage of the *Journal*'s overall front-page reporting can be considered deep accountability journalism than the *Times*'s or the *Post*'s. As detailed in Table 2–1, at the *Journal*, 4.03 percent of the front-page stories in the entire twenty-year sample were deep accountability reporting, compared with 3.80 percent at the *Post* and just 2.46 percent at the *New York Times*. It is important to use statistics in these comparisons rather than just raw figures because the *Journal* not only prints fewer stories per day on its front pages than its competitors, it prints less often than the *Times* and *Post*.[8] To explore the differences in the large papers' approaches to the watchdog role further, I will delve into the specific coverage at each one.

THE NEW YORK TIMES—SLOW TO BLOSSOM

The *New York Times* is often called "America's most revered newspaper,"[9] having won more Pulitzers and other top awards than any other. "The *New York Times* has been built and strengthened over generations by striving to be the best news operation in the world," says its current top editor, Dean Baquet.[10] So one might assume that the *Times* would come in first in this study in terms of deep accountability reporting. But the *Times* actually contained a *lower* percentage of deep accountability reporting in its front-page samples than the *Washington Post* and the *Wall Street Journal* overall. Although the *Times* did exceptionally well in public service journalism overall compared with the smaller newspapers, its front pages contained a lower percentage of "deep accountability" articles than the other two large papers studied here in four of the five months sampled. If there is a lesson to be gleaned from the *Times* accountability coverage, it is that newspapers can do only so much. If a publication like the *Times* sees itself as a "paper of record" and leans toward hard news coverage, then it will have fewer resources available for enterprise reporting than some of its competitors, which might not see their roles quite the same way.[11] The low quantities of original public policy journalism in the early study years imply that the *Times* was putting other kinds of reporting on its front page in the 1990s— namely, hard news. This is exactly what one would expect to see from a "paper of record." However, this started to change after the year 2000, when breaking news became so much easier to find on the Internet. This forced papers like the *Times* to differentiate themselves to keep their readers. As Baquet wrote in 2016:

> The digital news marketplace nudges us away from covering incremental developments—readers can find those anywhere in a seemingly endless online landscape. Instead, it favors hard-hitting "only-in-*The New York Times*" coverage: authoritative journalism and information readers can use to navigate their lives.[12]

As the environment for newspapers changed in the Internet era, it would seem that the *Times* content changed with it.

Table 2–2 presents an overview of the *NYT's* accountability reporting over the twenty years studied, showing extremely low quantities of original enterprise reporting on public policy issues in the early years. The samples show a shift away from breaking news and toward the *Times's* own original reporting on public policy over time, with the peak of original accountability reporting in the last study year, 2011. The total amount of original accountability reporting on government and policy issues rose over the study period, from a low of about one-tenth of front page content in 1991 up to one-third in 2011. The total amount of accountability reporting on the sampled front pages measured only about 10 percent during the 1991 and 1996 samples—much lower than those of the *Washington Post* and the *Journal* at the same time. The percentage of accountability reporting at the *Times* more than doubled in the 2001 and 2006 samples and then increased again by about a third in the 2011 sample.

The watchdog reporting at the *Times* in the study period was wide-ranging in terms of subject. A few stories were international in focus, but these usually focused on the role of the U.S. government or the U.S. military in a foreign policy issue. For example, a 2011 story, done in part with documents given to the *Times* by the organization Wikileaks, assessed the conditions of prisoners held at the U.S. military base in Guantánamo Bay, Cuba.[13] Other deep watchdog stories were nationally focused, like an

TABLE 2–2. Total Accountability Reporting (Classified as "Original Enterprise" and "Deep Accountability"), *New York Times*, Months of April, 1991–2011

New York Times	1991	1996	2001	2006	2011	Total
Total front-page stories	295	323	230	184	188	**1,220**
Total accountability stories	32	33	52	46	63	**226**
Simple/Deep	31 | 1	30 | 3	42 | 10	36 | 10	57 | 6	**196 | 30**
% Front-page accountability	**10.85%**	**10.22%**	**22.61%**	**25.00%**	**33.51%**	**18.52%**

investigation into income tax cuts by the George W. Bush administration.[14] Still others were local, like an analysis of the hiring of black officers by the New York City Police Department.[15] Several of those locally focused watchdog articles were parts of series, suggesting that when the *Times* found an important issue, it dedicated resources to investigating it properly and space to display the content.[16] Local elected officials were also popular subjects for investigation.[17] The *NYT* also did many investigative stories that looked into business, like a 2006 story on executive pay at Verizon and Verizon's use of outside compensation consultants.[18]

The data demonstrates how the *Times* was moving away from breaking news and toward original reporting, both regular enterprise and deep reporting, over the twenty-year study period. This finding confirms that the *Times* has adjusted its newsgathering strategy over time to put more of an emphasis on original enterprise reporting despite its tendency to go heavy on breaking news. "Now when people pick up the *New York Times*, they know a lot, they think they know a lot, about what happened yesterday," says Lelyveld. "The *Times* has to serve a broader purpose."[19] The largest increase in the number of enterprise stories about policy issues' being put on the *Times*'s front page happened in the 2001 sample, after the Internet came of age as a tool for sharing information. This increase suggests that the rise of the Internet as a source for spreading news caused the *Times* to focus less on breaking news and more on its own original stories. As with other papers, the *Times* seems increasingly to leave breaking news for the paper's web pages, leaving the front page of the print edition for more original journalism.

Part of the increase in the *Times*'s production of original accountability reporting seems to have been driven by staff change and a reorganization that strengthened the paper's ability to create deep dive reporting across departments. Lelyveld cites the arrival of Dean Baquet from the *Chicago Tribune* in 1990 and the creation of an investigative reporting unit under his aegis as key factors driving the rise of watchdog reporting at the *Times* during the study period. Lelyveld said he had recruited Baquet, who had won a Pulitzer Prize in 1988 at the *Tribune* for his watchdog reporting on the Chicago City Council. "He hadn't wanted to come to the *Times* because he didn't believe we cared enough about investigative reporting, and I just made a promise that we would keep that commitment and we did," explains Lelyveld.[20] He says that after Baquet's arrival, the *Times* assembled seventeen or eighteen people together in a conference room in its Washington bureau, all of whom were by some definition investigative reporters. All had previously worked for different units at the *Times*, under different editors. "And we developed what was for us a radical concept—

we had an investigative unit, and we could bring people together for major enterprise efforts," explains Lelyveld. "And a lot of that had to do with the recruitment of Dean Baquet." After a stint as editor of the *Los Angeles Times* beginning in 2000, Baquet later returned to the *Times* and eventually took Lelyveld's old position as executive editor in 2014.

Since becoming editor, Baquet has been highly engaged in keeping the business side of the *Times* strong, so that the editorial team gets the resources it needs to produce vibrant journalism. But the *Times* has seen its financial interests go up and down during the study period, and that seems to have had an effect on the amount of deep dive reporting it has been able to produce. In 1991, the entire New York Times Company's earnings were just $47 million, based on revenues of $1.7 billion,[21] and deep dive accountability was at a very low level. But the 1990s were a period of huge growth for the Times Company, fueled by a booming economy and the establishment of the *Times* as a national newspaper. "Before about 1990 or a little later, the *Times* was not available on the stands across the country except in a few major cities," recalls Lelyveld.[22] The paper's revenues grew as it began to publish and offer home delivery of a print paper throughout much of the nation, setting up its place as the national "paper of record." In addition, Lelyveld says the expansion of the *Times*'s distribution gave it an important cultural role as a central source of information for many Americans. "I think it's important for the society that there be one thing that you can be relatively sure that a high proportion of influential people and well-educated people have in common, will have seen in one sense or another," he says.[23] In 1995, the growth pushed company earnings up to $2.4 billion, 90 percent of it from the newspaper side of its business.[24] And the production of deep accountability reporting in the 1996 sample was up from its previous level.

The company became so flush that it was able to make expensive (and probably ill-advised) purchases like the 1993 acquisition of the *Boston Globe* and its affiliated media properties for a huge sum—some $1.1 billion.[25] By 2000, the Times Company had increased its earnings to more than $600 million per year based on revenues of $3.3 billion—about a twelve-times increase in only nine years. The 2001 study sample again correlates to the *NYT*'s strong financial situation at the time, with a large increase in deep dive accountability reporting over the sample in 1996.

But the slowdown in the media business after the turn of the millennium began to erode profits and cut into revenues. By 2003, revenues at the New York Times Company were down by more than one-third from 2000, as spending on such news events as the second Iraq war outpaced revenue growth. As profits started to fall, allegations of poor management began to fly, as did criticism of the *Times*'s management structure, which concentrates power in the hands of the longtime owners, the Ochs-Sulzberger family.[26] In 2006, the Times Company actually suffered a half-billion-dollar loss despite near-record revenues. Somehow, the *Times* was able to keep its production of deep accountability reporting high during the 2006 sample—probably because the job cuts started to hit only in the middle of 2006, when the paper eliminated 250 jobs.[27] There was another round of 100 job cuts in 2008.[28]

The financial problems spurred the company to take a $250 million loan from Mexican billionaire Carlos Slim Helu in 2009. Although the loan was controversial at the time,[29] it helped the paper stave off collapse and to restructure. The loan bought the paper time to sell off underperforming assets like the *Boston Globe* and boost its ad sales. The start of the paper's economic recovery correlates to the relatively strong level of deep dive accountability reporting in the 2011 sample, which dropped by about 12 percent from 2006, but certainly was not decimated by any stretch.

But *Times* insiders like Lelyveld worry about staffing levels' being adequate to foster deep dive reporting. News reports put the size of the *NYT*'s reporting staff in 2011 at 1,189—about the same size it was in 2003 and in the 1990s, according to Lelyveld.[30] However, he points out that the later staff figures include not only journalists and editors but also legions of workers in web production, who were few in his day—as the *Times* did not launch its website until 1996.[31] He suspects the number of reporters is likely lower now than in his day, when they numbered between 300 and 350. And that means fewer people are available to dig. "Between Albany, Hartford, and Trenton, the *New York Times* probably had a dozen state-house reporters in our region in the nineties. Today, I would imagine the number is more like three," posits Lelyveld.[32] Still, the *Times*'s staff is and has been the largest of any U.S. paper, considerably larger than the two other large papers studied here. The *Times* may have fewer reporters available to dig up news than a decade or two ago, but it still has plenty, meaning that despite staff cuts and financial straits, one would expect it to remain a high producer of deep accountability reporting.

It is also highly aggressive in its business strategy. Its 2 million paid digital subscriptions as of mid-2017 out of 3 million total weekday circulation[33] now bring in almost half the paper's digital income.[34] This suggests that the *NYT*'s strategy of wanting to be a truly national, "must-read" paper has worked well. In fact, the *Times* has more recently been positioning itself as must-reading not only for Americans, but for the entire world, as it boosts its international marketing and publishes editions in other languages, like Chinese.[35] As with any paper, the stronger the *Times* is economically, the more it can invest in its content.

The *Times* brings something else to the mix: high visibility. The role of the *Times* as a heavy influence on the national agenda is well documented.[36] Its front page is widely seen as a "pivotal gatekeeper of the public agenda."[37] As so many news organizations in the United States take their cues from the *Times* about what is important and newsworthy, there is likely an echo effect from the deep reporting done by the *NYT* being repeated in other media.[38] This would seem to be particularly true of investigations and watchdog reports being done on subjects of interest to a national, rather than a New York–area, audience. The *Times* also syndicates its content to news organizations all over the world, creating another way in which its reporting reaches consumers. Therefore, just looking at the amount of the content gives an underestimate of the *Times*'s effect through its accountability reporting. Although the *New York Times* was doing less deep accountability than some dailies studied for this book, its unique reach must be considered in one's assessing its overall role as a producer and distributor of public service journalism. It remains important.

THE *WASHINGTON POST*—THE PRIDE OF WOODWARD AND BERNSTEIN

The *Washington Post* occupies a special place in American journalism. The paper has been renowned for its watchdog reporting since its reporters Bob Woodward and Carl Bernstein broke open the Watergate scandal starting in 1972. "Doing investigative journalism—accountability and investigative journalism—is in the *Post*'s DNA and has been as long as any of us have been around in journalism," explains Marcus Brauchli, the newspaper's former top editor.[39] This study found that long after Watergate, the *Washington Post* remains more focused on accountability journalism than any other paper studied and, I would posit, any other paper in the country. The data collected shows it was the *Post*, not the larger *New York Times* or *Wall Street Journal*, that produced the most accountability reporting, in terms of percentage, of the nine newspapers studied, as well as the highest number of "deep accountability" reports. Moreover, the *Post* did all this with significantly less staff than its competitors.

The *Washington Post* not only topped the study in quantity of watchdog stories, but, by any objective standard, the quality of the reporting was extremely high. *Post* accountability articles were generally long, rich in quotes, and backed up by documents or data. The depth with which the *Post* dug into some stories seemed to go beyond that of any other newspapers studied here. For instance, the paper conducted hundreds of interviews for a 1996 investigation into the life of the "Unabomber," Ted Kaczynski.[40] Similarly, the paper's look into an important local news story, how two new sports stadiums came to Maryland, took more than fifty interviews and a review of government documents.[41]

The *Washington Post* was able to achieve all this by making accountability journalism a priority. "We not only didn't cut back on [accountability reporting], we sort of put further emphasis on it," explains Brauchli. "That's how you differentiate yourself."[42] The *Post* also focused its public service journalism on its core mission—covering the capital better than anyone else. Much as the *New York Times* might like to consider itself the most important paper in Washington, the *Post* is widely considered the dominant news source in the nation's capital.[43]

Given its dominance in the Washington, D.C., area, one would expect the *Post* to be focused on being a watchdog over the federal government, and the data collected here shows that to be the case. Whereas the *New York Times* stories examined focused primarily on the work of elected officials in the New York area, the *Post* stories generally covered national figures, including the White House chief of staff,[44] the comptroller of the currency,[45] and then–presidential candidate Senator Bob Dole.[46] Another frequent accountability topic at the *Post* was the U.S. military, including its operations in places like Guantánamo Bay[47] and Iraq.[48] The *Post* also examined numerous national issues in its articles, requiring trips outside the Washington area, including stories on food safety[49] and sexual harassment.[50] But it took on numerous state and local issues as well, including education[51] and crime.[52] The *Post*'s local coverage also included its keeping an eye on such infamous figures as former Washington, D.C., Mayor Marion Barry.[53]

As shown by the results summarized in Table 2–3, the total amount of accountability reporting found in the *Washington Post*'s front-page samples evinces a much higher sustained interest in public service journalism than at the *New York Times*. The amount of front-page accountability reporting at the *WaPo* not only started high, it then rose by more than 60 percent over the length of the study.

TABLE 2–3. Total Front-Page Accountability Reporting, *Washington Post*, Months of April, 1991–2011

Washington Post	1991	1996	2001	2006	2011	Total/Avg.
Total front-page stories	199	197	213	184	155	948
Total accountability stories	55	61	77	74	68	335
Simple/Deep	52 | 3	54 | 7	68 | 9	69 | 5	56 | 12	299 | 36
% Front-page accountability	27.64%	30.96%	36.15%	40.22%	43.87%	35.34%

The increase in this public service reporting was not only profound, but it was slow and steady over the study period, from 27 percent front-page accountability at the start to 43 percent at the end, suggesting that there was a long-term commitment by management to dedicating resources to public service journalism. The increase in accountability reporting also suggests that the *Post* was, over time, becoming less dependent on breaking news and more interested in its own original reporting. This would seem to be part of a strategy that emphasizes the *Post*'s unique view of Washington as its main selling point. The *Post*, it seems, had a large taste for its own original stories on government and public policy going back to the beginning of the study period—not just in the digital era.

The *Washington Post* seems particularly committed to the deep forms of accountability reporting. The percentage of deep accountability stories about governmental actors grew over the study period from a low of just 1 percent in the 1991 sample to nearly 6 percent in the 2011 sample. Nonetheless, the *Post* did not ignore businesses and other nongovernmental actors, which accounted for almost 1 percent of its sampled front-page content. In addition, *Post* stories studied also included investigations into such nongovernmental players as Boeing[54] and Mitsubishi.[55]

What is most surprising about these results is that the *Post* was able to maintain and even expand its commitment to public service journalism even through incredibly difficult financial straits. Although the overall health of the entire Washington Post Company was relatively good during most the study period because of its non-newspaper holdings, the financial health of the *Washington Post* newspaper was absolutely dire. The *Post* was walloped by the world financial crisis. After seeing relatively small profits from 2000 to 2007, the *Post* incurred more than $440 million in losses between 2008 and 2012—most of it in 2008 and 2009, according to the figures in the company's annual reports.[56] The *Post*'s print ad revenue shrank by 60 percent between 2001 and 2012, say the reports, and digital revenue did not come anywhere close to making up the loss in print ad income. Adding to the overall shortfall was a drop in subscription revenue. The *Post* was losing readers overall and was relatively slow to get its readers to move to digital subscriptions.

For many years, the Post Company's non-newspaper subsidiaries were able to fill the corporation's coffers, softening the blow that the economy had on the *Washington Post* and the company's other newspaper holdings, most of them small weeklies. A major part of the Post Company's income during the years covered by this study came from the highly profitable educational company Kaplan, Inc., best known for its SAT and other test preparation courses and which has more recently branched out into online university–level education. Kaplan, Inc., had until 2010 been a "cash cow" for the company, bringing in revenues that subsidized other operations—like newspapers.[57] But when Kaplan, Inc., was no longer able to generate the company's cash in light of increased federal scrutiny by the Obama administration, the *Post*'s controlling family sought to sell the paper.[58]

Faced with possible bankruptcy, the Post Company sold the *Washington Post* newspaper and the rest of its newspaper division to Jeffrey P. Bezos, the billionaire founder of the Amazon online store, in 2013. The industry-shaking move was widely interpreted as the controlling Graham family's attempt to save the *Post* by putting it into the hands of a deep-pocketed owner who could invest in its future. "We weren't looking to close the *Post* or to a forced sale, but we finally saw that this is what was best for the paper," Washington Post Company chairman Donald Graham explained at the time.[59] The full evaluation of Bezos's commitment to deep account-ability reporting will be left to another study, but the early signs are deeply encouraging. "Listen to what Bezos says, or watch where he puts his money and directs his focus, and you can see how he's starting to overlay the brilliance of Amazon onto the scaffolding of the *Washington Post*," con-cludes the *Columbia Journalism Review*.[60] The *Post* added more than one hundred staffers in Bezos's first year and started all kinds of new proj-ects—many of them technological—boding well for the future.[61]

The *Post* could use the extra hands. Staffing levels at the *Post* had been falling for years, even while the newspaper division was profitable. Com-pany reports say the total number of *Post* staff dropped by about a quarter in this century alone, from 690 in 2002 down to 536 in 2012, including 77 digital positions that had not existed before. Discounting those, it is fair to say that about one-third of the *Post* jobs that existed in 2002 ceased to exist over the next 10 years. These figures suggest that throughout the study period, the *Washington Post* had a staff that was much smaller than that of the *New York Times*. The fact that the *Post* maintained its deep account-ability reporting at such high levels suggests a stand by management to make public service journalism a priority, and heroic efforts by *Post* staff members to make watchdog reporting a reality.

The *Post* also trimmed back its bureaus located internationally, domesti-cally, and locally during the study period. On the foreign front, editors cut the *Post*'s presence by more than a quarter, from twenty-one international bureaus in 2002 down to fifteen in 2014, according to Post Company annual reports. Many of those *Post* international bureaus also fell from multiple correspondents down to one.[62] Surprisingly, these job cuts did not seem to lower much the amount of accountability reporting on foreign affairs, according to the data collected by this study. The percentage of front-page accountability reports on international affairs fell from about 15 percent in the 2001 sample to 13 percent in 2006 and 2011. And as the number of *Post*'s correspondents working abroad fell, the percentage of accountability reports sampled that focused on foreign officials actually went up a bit, from about 14 percent in 2001 to more than 17 percent in the 2011 sample. This would seem to fall in line with the larger finding of this study that editors can continue the flow of public service journalism despite job losses.

What would seem to be more relevant to this study is the elimination of the paper's domestic bureaus. During the depth of the paper's financial woes in 2009, the *Post*'s management—after having expanded the number of domestic correspondents in the preceding decade—decided to close all of the paper's domestic bureaus. The *Post* went from five offices around the country in 2002 to seven in 2005, according to its annual report, before closing them all in 2010. The point was to save money and perhaps even save the paper by refashioning the *Post* not as a national newspaper but as the "paper of record" for Washington, D.C., alone. "We are not a national news organization of record serving a general audience. Nor are we a wire service or cable channel," Brauchli said at the time of the closures. "The *Post*'s strength is to report issues through a 'Washington prism.'"[63] Not many people bought that reasoning, least of all the *Post*'s influential media critic Howard Kurtz, who called the closure "the clearest sign yet of the newspaper's shrinking horizons in an era of diminished resources."[64]

But when interviewed for this book, Brauchli said the move to close the domestic bureaus had been misunderstood. "At that time, we were under immense pressure to reduce costs," he recalled.[65] He said that the financial pressures forced the paper to review its operations from top to bottom:

> What we really needed was to figure out what value the *Washington Post* could have, and ensure that we were focused on doing what the *Washington Post* needed to do, which at that moment was retain and build on its authority in politics, policy, and issues of consequence to people in Washington.[66]

To do so, Brauchli shifted resources, refocusing on the *Post*'s central mission of serving the capital. "We just didn't need to be producing our version of general news stories from three places in the country," he explains.[67] He says that the paper did end up keeping some staff outside Washington, including people covering sports and the United Nations in New York, which editors did feel added to the paper's overall editorial mission. The data collected by this survey suggests that the *Post*'s accountability coverage turned somewhat more Washington-focused over time, with increasing numbers of stories about the president, Congress, and the federal bureaucracy.

Just as disturbing to some members of the staff was the *Post*'s decision to save money by closing all its local bureaus except the ones in the Virginia and Maryland state capitals. The *WaPo* went from twelve local bureaus in 2002 to just two in 2014. No staff members were cut, but the move saved on expensive office rent and, in the words of local editor Vernon Loeb, to get "out of our offices, including the bureaus, and out in the world where people are that we are writing about. News doesn't happen in bureaus. It happens out in the world."[68] Although there were no job cuts, the data suggests that simply closing the bureaus still led to fewer accountability reports addressing state and local government. The percentage of reports with a focus on state or local government was less than half as many in the 2006 sample as they had been in 1996. The cuts seemed to have serious effects on the *WaPo*'s coverage of state government. The 2011 sample had rather robust coverage of local government, including the one in Washington, D.C., but no stories at all focusing on state legislatures, state agencies, state police, or state courts.

That said, the data collected for this research suggests that the *WaPo* editors' strategy to use resources strategically paid off, allowing the paper's limited resources to be funneled into accountability reporting rather successfully. Despite jettisoning staff, losing money, and closing bureaus, the *Post* produced more deep accountability reporting overall than either of the other newspapers in the large-paper cohort, and more than any paper in the entire study. In particular, it is telling that the single highest output of "deep accountability" reporting came in the 2011 sample, when the *Post* was arguably in its worst position financially during the study period and had the smallest staff. "It was clearly conveyed that we wanted to put an emphasis on original journalism that you couldn't get elsewhere because that has value . . . for the newspaper and has digital value," Brauchli says.[69] He says that even though the paper was feeling financial pressure at the time, it purposefully did not cut back on the kind of deep reporting that he and his colleagues believed was central to its mission. This is typical of the strategy we will see in the medium-sized-newspaper group—to double down on the most meaningful reporting, even though it is expensive and hard—because it is what truly serves the community.

But have *Post* readers responded to the uptick in deep accountability journalism? Unfortunately, the focus on public service journalism has not seemed to drive up print circulation, at least not during the years studied by this project. Except for a tiny uptick in 2013, *Washington Post* circulation dropped every year from 2000 through 2014. Circulation peaked for the daily edition in 1993 at about 830,00 and on Sundays in 1992 at 1.16 million.[70] As of late 2016, *Post* circulation had fallen by half from its peak.[71] Of course, circulation might have dropped even more without the increase in accountability reporting, but a loss of half its print circulation would be devastating to most newspapers.

However, *Post* digital readership has gone up significantly over time. The *Post* was relatively slow to adopt a paywall, doing so long after its competitors had done so. But it has been making up for lost time since being purchased by one of the most tech-savvy entrepreneurs in the world. "Since Bezos bought it, traffic to washingtonpost.com has more than doubled. When it briefly beat out the New York *Times* in November [2016], to celebrate, the *Post* ran house ads [self-promotional advertisements in its own pages] proclaiming itself 'the new publication of record.'"[72] Although the Bezos purchase and its aftermath came too late to affect the figures gathered for this study, the *Post* seems to have adopted a much more aggressive digital strategy under its new owner than it had during the study period, which is driving up online readership and, in tandem, online revenue. This more successful digital strategy bodes well for the *Post*'s approach to accountability reporting in the future, as it requires funding and an audience to develop maximum reach.

Media experts and newspaper executives are watching closely to see whether Bezos will continue to invest in the *Washington Post* so that it can continue to expand its reporting, and whether he will spur the organization to improve its digital presence. Steve Hills, the past president of the *Washington Post* newspaper, says that Bezos has been trying to focus on the *Post*'s long-term prospects as a technology company, not just as a news provider: "He is asking the question of: 'What can you do to have a great digital audience 10 years, 20 years from now?'" Mr. Hills said. "Under previous ownership, the very reasonable question we were asking was: 'How do we make money in the next two to three years?' This different orientation opens up a wide range of new opportunities," he added. "That's the interesting part of the story."[73]

This emphasis on technology has led to some outside-the-box thinking at the *Post* when it comes to upping readership. Bezos approved offering a free *Post* digital subscription to the paid subscribers of some other non-competing American newspapers starting in 2014.[74] By mid-2015, that program had grown from a handful of American newspapers outside the capital region to more than 250 national and international news organizations.[75] Bezos is also experimenting with all kinds of new digital partnerships.[76] The paper is also offering its app pre-loaded onto Amazon Fire tablets, leading to more subscriptions.

The *Post*'s role as a pariah in the Trump era is also likely to bring it high readership. After all, this was a paper that Trump banned from some campaign events because he objected to the critical lens through which the paper covered his candidacy. Bezos has deep pockets, and buying the *Post* could be more than an act of vanity if he uses some of that money to keep strengthening the paper's newsgathering ability, to help it keep its focus on accountability reporting in the capital and beyond.

THE *WALL STREET JOURNAL*—WATCHING THE GOVERNMENT, NOT JUST BUSINESS

The *Wall Street Journal* holds a unique spot in American journalism as the dominant national business-oriented newspaper. Founded in 1889 by business journalists Charles Dow ("a reserved and tenacious reporter who took notes on his shirt cuffs") and Edward Jones ("a high-spirited bon vivant with a knack for analyzing financial reports"),[77] the *Journal* has risen to become a necessity for corporate Americans. Financial journalists still consider it the most influential media outlet on financial news.[78] The paper's success would prove that "reliable financial information was the fundamental currency of almost every part of life, from building railroads to buying kitchen sinks."[79] Its high and steady circulation demonstrates its importance as a news source. It was also widely available for sale and delivery in print form around the country during the study period, which helped to cement its position as a must-read newspaper for people in business.

But the *Journal* hasn't been content with being just a financial newspaper. It bills itself as something much bigger: "the gold-standard of journalism . . . the industry leader delivering the most crucial news of the day, insightful opinion and fair-minded analysis."[80] Its quest for profits and influence has led the paper to make fundamental changes in its content since the 1990s. The quest for new readers beyond the business elite spurred the development of a wider range of content at the *Journal* throughout the study period. After expanding into a two- and then three-section paper in the 1980s, the *WSJ* added numerous new features and sections in the 1990s and 2000s aimed at attracting new readers. These new features went beyond mainline financial reporting into subjects like food, fashion, and technology.

The changes have accelerated since the purchase in 2007 of the newspaper and its parent company, Dow Jones, by the business mogul Rupert Murdoch's News Corporation. The highly controversial $5.6 billion sale resulted from a deep split in the controlling Bancroft family, descendants of publisher Clarence Walker Barron, who had acquired Dow Jones from its founders in 1902. The *Washington Post* called Murdoch's purchase a "coup," even though News Corp. had to pay two-thirds more than the prevailing value for the company.[81] Those studying the *Journal* have noted that since the News Corp. purchase, Murdoch "is seeking to shift the *Journal*'s coverage to include much more politics, more elections, more general government activity. In other words, Murdoch is 'De-Financializing' the paper."[82] Some media analysts have speculated that Murdoch would like the *Journal* to unseat the *New York Times* as the national "paper of record."[83]

The *Wall Street Journal*'s attempt to broaden its appeal is reflected in its accountability content. In the early study years, before the Internet came into widespread usage, the *Journal*'s accountability reporting focused mainly on businesses and other nongovernmental actors that play a role in public policy issues, rather than on the government itself. But that all changed in the later study years, when the *WSJ* began to expand its public service journalism aggressively into examinations of the government as well as business. This suggests that the *Journal*'s quest to make itself a more widely read newspaper had an unexpected spillover effect, turning the paper into a more vital watchdog over the government.

Of course, the *WSJ* has investigations in its DNA, too. The legendary Bernard Kilgore, who served as managing editor from 1941 to 1967, was responsible for creating the newspaper's inquisitive culture by insisting that a long explanatory piece appear on the front page daily. This "forced reporters to ask deeper questions, not merely about momentary events but about ongoing situations and trends—the kind of news a business reader could use."[84] This tradition of original enterprise reporting is reflected in the results for this study, which show the *Journal* to have the highest percentage of front-page deep accountability content of all nine newspapers studied.

How can the *WSJ* manage to police both government and business? Marcus Brauchli, who worked at the *Journal* from 1984 to 2008 and was its top editor from 2007 to 2008, says that the newspaper is broad and opportunistic in its approach to accountability reporting. Brauchli says its staff approach investigative work differently from the staff of the *Washington Post*, to which he moved in 2008:

> They have very different cultures. The *Post* had put a premium on a strong, pure investigative unit. And their focus is very much around accountability journalism involving government, which is a natural and obvious place for the *Post* to put its energy. The *Journal* tends to do investigative journalism more opportunistically, less systematically. It looks for strong stories in any

of its core areas of coverage. And there's no zone that the *Journal* wouldn't be aggressive in going after.[85]

The data confirms that the *Journal*'s appetite for accountability reporting is not only broad but also steady. The percentage of accountability reports on the front page as defined by this study is almost the same in 2011 as it was in 1991, with relatively high accountability output in the intervening years. The data suggests that the *WSJ* is willing to throw its considerable weight around to ferret out a good story wherever it sees one, to the benefit of its readers.

The *Journal* may not have produced the highest raw number of accountability stories in the months studied (that was the *Washington Post*), but it did produce the highest percentage of stories with sustained digging. The data collected shows that the five samples of the *Wall Street Journal* had a lower overall percentage of accountability journalism than the *Washington Post*, but significantly more than the *New York Times*. As shown by the figures in Table 2–4, the *Journal* also had the highest overall percentage of "deep accountability" reports of the nine papers studied, just nosing out the *Washington Post* by a few hundredths of 1 percent.

That three in ten front-page stories in the *Journal* sample overall cover public policy issues in an enterprising fashion is a strong result. Even in its worst year sampled, 1996, about a quarter of the *WSJ*'s front page could be considered original accountability reporting. Of course, as a large and relatively rich newspaper, the *Journal* has the staffing necessary to ensure a steady flow of public service journalism. Although staffing levels are not public, interviews and press reports suggest that staffing for the *Journal* held steady at about 750 reporters and editors between 1991 and 2008 before falling after the world financial crisis hit.[86]

Not surprisingly, the *Journal* is much more focused on producing accountability journalism that involves businesses and corporations than the other two large newspapers studied. This only underlines that there is too little deep investigative reporting about business and other nongovern-

TABLE 2–4. Total Accountability Reporting, *Wall Street Journal*, Months of April, 1991–2011

Wall Street Journal	1991	1996	2001	2006	2011	Total/Avg.
Total front-page stories	78	86	85	95	103	447
Total accountability stories	25	21	25	26	33	130
Simple/Deep	24 | 1	19 | 2	20 | 5	21 | 5	28 | 5	112 | 18
% Front-page accountability	**32.05%**	**24.42%**	**29.41%**	**27.37%**	**32.04%**	**29.08%**

mental actors at most American newspapers. Yet the *Journal* has hardly abdicated the watchdog role with regard to government. Table 2–5 summarizes the breakdown of the *Wall Street Journal*'s "deep accountability" reporting, showing that it began to spread its attention from business to government starting with the 2001 sample.

The *WSJ* ran "deep accountability" stories about nongovernmental actors during each study month examined. It carried between one and three of these kinds of investigative pieces per sample, or more than 2.22 percent of its front-page stories overall. This represents a significant investment of reporter time and resources in reporting on how businesses and corporations affect public policy issues, far beyond what any other paper surveyed was able to accomplish. The data also details how the *Journal* changed its attention in the digital era from digging into business alone in its deep accountability reporting to addressing government as well. In the first two samples, no "deep accountability" stories at all were produced that had the government as their main actor. But in the later samples, slightly more of the "deep accountability" stories produced addressed governmental rather than nongovernmental actors. This seems indicative of the larger changes going on at the *Journal* at the time, as it morphed from a purely business paper to a more general one.

The topics covered by the *Journal*'s deep stories on nongovernmental actors can be classified into three main types. The first is investigations of individual businesses. An example of this type of article was published on April 25, 1996, when the *Journal* examined how the British pharmaceutical company Boots got into conflict with American researchers whose research work it was funding.[87] Relations soured when the researchers' results started to go against Boots' products. Other investigations of this type

TABLE 2–5. Nongovernmental/Governmental Focus, *Wall Street Journal*, Months of April, 1991–2011

Wall Street Journal	1991	1996	2001	2006	2011	Total/Avg.
Total # "Simple enterprise" stories	24	19	20	21	28	112
Nongovernmental	21	15	17	16	18	87
Governmental	3	4	3	5	10	25
% Governmental "simple enterprise"	12.50%	21.00%	15.00%	24.00%	36.00%	22.32%
Total # "Deep accountability" stories	1	2	5	5	5	18
Nongovernmental	1	2	3	1	3	10
Governmental	0	0	2	4	2	8
% Governmental "Deep accountability"	0.00%	0.00%	40.00%	80.00%	40.00%	44.44%

addressed British Petroleum's relations with the Russian government[88] and the safety of Amoco drilling rigs in Alaska.[89] A second genre of *Journal* investigation examines broad sectors of business and covers multiple firms. An article of this type was an excellent *Journal* investigation into the illegal worldwide trade in mercury, one of the world's most toxic substances.[90] The reporter traced the trade through a chain of companies, brokers, and smugglers. The reporting took him from legal mercury recycling in Maine to under-the-counter sales of contraband mercury deep in the Brazilian rainforest. In a similar vein, the *Journal* investigated whether firms that claimed to produce non–genetically modified food actually did so.[91] Through independent lab testing, the *WSJ* ascertained that many of the foods marketed as free of genetically modified ingredients actually had them. Through this kind of independent analysis—which was not cheap—the *Journal* performed a valuable public service. The third type of investigation undertaken by the *WSJ* is the re-creation of an event, where new details are brought to light through the *Journal's* reporting. A story of this genre was the April 4, 2011, article about the murder of seven United Nations workers at a compound in Mazar-E-Sharif, Afghanistan.[92] The article stated that the reporters reconstructed the events "based on unreleased videos, interviews with demonstrators and the U.N.'s own recounting of events."[93] These kinds of investigations employ a wide range of reporting techniques to create an atmosphere of scrutiny.

But all these investigations into nongovernmental actors do not mean that the *Journal* passed on acting as a watchdog over the government, for it certainly did. It covered a very broad array of governmental actors in its accountability reports in the study period, but finance seems to be the running theme through much of its watchdog journalism. The *Journal* held members of Congress responsible for their financial dealings.[94] It watched over campaign finance.[95] It assessed whether government agencies were being fair to businesses they regulated.[96] But not all its watchdog stories dealt with money, like its exposé into how the U.S. military edged into domestic surveillance after 9/11.[97]

These strong results, particularly in the "deep" reporting category, were accompanied—or engendered—by a strong financial situation at the *Wall Street Journal* itself. Unlike the *Washington Post*, which saw its circulation erode during the study period, the *Journal's* circulation grew in almost every year. From 1991 to 2002, *Journal* circulation hovered around 1.8 million copies.[98] By 2003, circulation was more than 2 million copies a day. The *Journal* also seems to have benefited from an aggressive stance on paywalls. It was the first major U.S. newspaper to institute paid digital subscriptions, in 1997. "People who read the *Wall Street Journal* tend to think of it as an essential source of information for their economic life. And the *Journal* has from the very beginning taken the view that it offers great value to people and they should pay for it," says Brauchli, who worked at the *Journal* during the imposition of the paywall.[99] As of mid-2017, the *WSJ* said it had more than 1.27 million digital subscribers.[100]

The *Journal*'s circulation has increased slightly since the sale to News Corp., and this study suggests its production of accountability reporting has also remained solid. But that doesn't mean there aren't concerns for the future. When News Corp. acquired Dow Jones, staff members at the newspaper were nervous about the new bosses. "The once-mighty, staid, studiously gray, independent *Wall Street Journal* was now a first cousin to Fox ('Fair and Balanced') News, Bart Simpson, the London daily *Sun*'s Page Three titty displays, and the deliberately outrageous *New York Post*."[101] Several properties at News Corp.—particularly the cable station Fox News Channel in the United States—have been shown by studies to reflect the conservative Republican preferences of their chief executive:

> The second distinctive feature of News Corporation is that, as a corporate entity, it holds long-standing policies towards major matters of public interest and it campaigns for those policies. It has policies that are often announced by its CEO and that affect the news and comment it publishes.[102]

But after the purchase, Dow Jones agreed to form a "special committee" that would ensure the newspaper's editorial independence. The special committee, which still exists, includes retired news executives and academics.

The jump in total public affairs journalism reports on the front page from 27 percent in 2006 to 32 percent in 2011—a rise of about a third—suggests that the *Journal* is continuing to dedicate significant resources to original reporting on the government and policy under Murdoch. This is good news. That the number of investigations jumped under News Corp. suggests that the *Journal* remains committed to applying scrutiny to the business world under its new owners. This is very important, as few papers have the resources and focus to match the *Journal* in the investigatory realm.

Given the limited scope of this study, it is difficult to determine whether the *Journal*'s commitment to watchdog reporting will continue to change under News Corp. Still, it is worth noting that despite a drop in the number of "deep watchdog" stories at the *WSJ* from 2006 to 2011, the paper seemed far more committed to deep public affairs reporting in 2011 than it had been in 1991 or 1996, when its front-page samples had no "deep watchdog" reporting at all. The *Journal* bears watching, to make sure it keeps its eye on business conduct. Other papers are keeping watch over businesses and corporations, but none of them have quite the reach or cachet as the *Wall Street Journal.*

CONCLUSIONS ABOUT THE LARGE NEWSPAPER GROUP

There can be little doubt that the three large newspapers studied are major producers of accountability reporting and that all consider deep accountability reporting to be a key part of their missions. Despite drops in deep reporting output at the *Times* and the *Journal* in the 2011 sample, the three papers still did far more deep accountability reporting in 2011 than they did in the early study years. This would seem to allay fears that deep watchdog and deep investigative reporting is dying out in this era of tight money and small staffs. In fact, the results of the study suggest that the papers in this group remain the most likely to take on accountability reporting involving federal government agencies and multinational corporations. For that reason alone, the ability of large newspapers to take on accountability reporting remains critically important. In addition, much of the most important accountability stories done by the *Times* and *Post* are syndicated and so appear on the front pages of countless other newspapers across the country. This, too, suggests a unique and important role being played by the large newspaper group.

But that said, it is difficult to determine how the situation for accountability reporting at each paper would look had I been able to extend the study another five years to April 2016 and beyond. Looking at the three papers studied in the large newspaper group, we can see that each seemed to be on a different trajectory in terms of deep accountability reporting coming out of the study period in 2011.

At the *New York Times*, the trajectory from 2006 to 2011 was downward, as both the raw number and the percentage of watchdog stories on the front page dropped. Although the *Times* still produces a healthy amount of accountability reporting overall, any fall in its output of deep reporting is troublesome, as the *Times* does so much to set the national news agenda. Luckily, its current editor, Dean Baquet, has a strong track record of encouraging deep accountability reporting, and my impression as a subscriber to that newspaper is that it still turns out several well-researched deep dive accountability stories each month.

At the *Wall Street Journal*, the output of deep accountability reporting seemed quite steady in the twenty-first century, with five deeply reported stories in each of the samples studied between 2001 and 2011. But it remains unclear whether there will be any effect on the creation of accountability reporting under News Corp. management. The role of the *Journal* as a watchdog over big business remains unparalleled. Although the other papers also undertake investigations into large companies, this study suggests that deep investigative reporting about nongovernmental actors is underproduced by American newspapers. That means it is essential that the *Journal* maintain its leading role as a vigilant force monitoring the world of big business.

And at the *Washington Post*, the trajectory since 2006 has been upward, with more than twice as many "deep watchdog" reports in the 2011 sample as in 2006. Early signs are that the Bezos era will be a good one for the paper, as staff has expanded and new initiatives have been launched under the *Post*'s new owner. As we shall see in the next chapter, the cohort of medium-sized metropolitan dailies has also jumped into deep accountability reporting with both feet.

Whatever these large papers may or may not have been doing in 2016, they play a particularly important role as watchdogs over the government during a controversial presidential administration. Although Donald Trump tried to bully the *New York Times* and the *Washington Post* during the presidential campaign—going so far as to ban *Post* reporters from some campaign events—the newspapers were so large and powerful that they were able to withstand the pressure. These giants of the American press set the tone for the rest of the media when they dig in their heels and insist that they be allowed to perform the watchdog role envisioned by our nation's founders. If they fight back against attempts to sideline or discredit their reporting, they perform a service to all of the American media by discouraging future attacks.

It is worth ending this discussion with a brief mention of the rising amount of anonymous sourcing in these three newspapers' accountability coverage. In order to get more accountability stories, the three papers—particularly the *Post* and the *Journal*—seem to have loosened up over time on their rules for using anonymous sources. The *WaPo* had the highest percentage of unnamed sources in its sampled articles of the nine newspapers studied, with more than 13 percent anonymous sources in its accountability stories overall. The *Washington Post*'s use of high numbers of unnamed sources over the study years makes sense, given its position covering the nation's capital. As famed Watergate reporter Bob Woodward put it, "When you are reporting on inside the White House, the Supreme Court, the CIA or the Pentagon, you tell me how you're going to get stuff on the record. Look at the good reporting out of any of those institutions—it's not on the record."[103] That said, the figure for unnamed sources at the *Post* still remains much higher than those of the other newspapers studied here.

The *Journal* also had large numbers, with 6.3 percent unnamed sources overall. The *WSJ* also had a significant jump in anonymous sourcing after the News Corp. purchase, as unnamed sources increased from about 5 percent of people quoted in the 2006 sample to almost 13 percent in 2011. This raises questions about the newspaper's approach to anonymous sourcing in the Murdoch era. Somehow, the *New York Times* managed to keep its use of anonymous sources down considerably. Its samples contained only about 3 percent anonymous quotes overall, though it, too, saw its use of unnamed sources more than double from 2006 to 2011.

This increase in anonymous sourcing at all three papers in the 2011 sample seems to confirm scholars' earlier conclusions about sources' becoming more reluctant to speak on the record in the digital age, when it is simpler than ever to trace comments to their source.[104] This makes sense, but the use of unnamed sources has both benefits and drawbacks. While many accountability stories require the information streams enabled by anonymity, readers generally distrust information that is not attributed.[105] Newspapers—and not just the large ones studied here—would be well served to enunciate their policies about anonymous sources and then stick to their own rules. The *New York Times* has a written policy on anonymous sourcing that is easy for its readers and reporters to find and easy to understand.[106] It also seems to be enforced, which is likely one of the reasons why the *Times* uses far fewer anonymous sources than the other two large papers studied here. The *Post* also has a written policy, but its own ombudsman suggested it was not often followed. Calling the over-use of anonymous sources a "problem" and "endemic," he said, "Reporters should be blamed. But the solution must come in the form of unrelenting enforcement by editors, starting with those at the top."[107] On the other hand, I had great difficulty finding the *Wall Street Journal*'s policy on anonymous sources. I could not locate it through Internet searches, and no one at Dow Jones would share the policy with me, though they confirmed that it does exist. The *New York Times* may have come in third in this study in terms of quantity of deep accountability reporting, but I would put it first in its approach to anonymous sourcing. In an era when the president pushes back against media criticism, sources are likely to demand even more anonymity when presenting information that is critical of the government. This means that newspapers would be well served by reviewing their policies on unnamed sources and applying them consistently, to help manage the tension inherent in getting on-the-record information for watchdog stories.

CHAPTER 3

The Workhorse of the Watchdogs

The next group of newspapers studied, the metropolitan dailies, are vibrant producers of public service journalism.[1] Their editors see original watchdog stories as being at the very core of what makes the papers a value to their communities. "We've learned that our readers don't want us to be frivolous or silly or working on something that's not of consequence," explains Kevin Riley, editor of the *Atlanta Journal-Constitution*. "They want the most important stories on the front page. They want a newspaper that tells them what they need to know, that makes sense out of their world, and that demands high standards from the community's leaders and its important institutions."[2] These medium-sized dailies, the workhorses of the watchdogs in this study, give concrete evidence that accountability reporting is not only alive and well, but also that it continues to be valued by its audience.

The four members of this sample group of papers—the *Atlanta Journal-Constitution* (*AJC*), *Minneapolis Star Tribune* (*StarTrib* or *Strib*), *The Denver Post*, and the *Albany Times Union* (*ATU*)—have over time evolved considerably in terms of content, and their paths illustrate the challenges that metropolitan newspapers face today in trying to keep the watchdog tradition alive. Three of the four newspapers in this group created little accountability reporting at the start of the study but grew to be large producers by the end. The fourth one started as a huge producer of public service journalism, but turned out lower quantities as budgets became tighter and the staff leaner. The stories behind those contrasting trajectories provide telling contrasts between the larger and smaller newspapers in this diverse group and suggest larger lessons for how mid-sized newspapers can grapple with issues tied to producing meaningful accountability journalism.

More specifically, the *Atlanta Journal-Constitution*, the *Star Tribune*, and *The Denver Post* bear little resemblance to their previous incarnations in 1991 or 1996 in terms of content, when the emphasis was on breaking news. The samples from 1991 and 1996 had almost no watchdog reporting, almost no investigative journalism, and little original enterprise reporting. They contained mostly breaking news, either written by staff or reprinted from wire services. To be honest, some of the front pages I examined in these newspapers in the early study years contained few stories that would compel readers to pay for a copy. The *Journal-Constitution*, especially, was particularly weak and did a poor job of doing anything in the Atlanta region beyond basic headline news.

But that all changed over time, as these papers rediscovered what they had to do well in the digital age to keep their readers. Today, these three particular medium-sized newspapers are vibrant multimedia organizations that dedicate a relatively large percentage of their front pages to accountability reporting, both state and local, and occasionally federal. They have expanded public service journalism, despite the financial challenges. They win prizes for their work, and their reputations are solid. And circulation losses have either slowed or turned around at these papers as their content has moved into more enterprise reporting and a greater emphasis on accountability journalism. They demonstrate that newspapers *can* overcome limited resources if their editors make accountability reporting a high priority and put muscle into their mission—and that readers do respond.

But the fourth newspaper, the *Albany Times Union*, followed a slightly different and more complicated path. It started the study period as a high producer of accountability reporting, taking advantage of its location in the capital of the state of New York. While it remained a relatively large producer of public service journalism over the length of the study, it never again attained the high output in subsequent years that it had in the 1991 sample. The *Times Union* didn't taper down; its production of accountability reporting actually vacillated over the study period quite significantly as the paper grappled with resource issues and a migration of its readership from print to digital. Though it still managed to produce large numbers of accountability stories in the later study years, the *Times Union* staff had to work harder to do so. The paper also moved aggressively into online publication and had to spend crucial resources on establishing a vibrant web presence. The *Times Union*'s experience suggests that even newspapers that are committed to watchdog reporting can face considerable struggles to turn their aspirations into reality in this world of scant resources. The *Times Union* had strong support for accountability journalism from both its editor and the corporation that owns it, like the other three papers in this group. But it is so much smaller than the Atlanta, Minneapolis, and Denver papers that the *Times Union*'s very high aspirations could not always be achieved. Even when a newspaper is large enough to anchor its community, it seems, its size and resource levels still matter.

MORE ENTERPRISING, DESPITE CHALLENGES

These four papers worked to keep up a commitment to public service journalism despite their facing significant financial issues in recent years, as falling revenue from shrinking ad sales led to cuts in staffing and lower newsgathering budgets. The *Star Tribune* might be considered the worst-off financially of the four, as it actually had to file for Chapter 11 bankruptcy protection in January 2009 after earnings tumbled. *The Denver Post* also sustained huge losses before and after the turn of the millennium because of competition from another Denver daily, the *Rocky Mountain News*. The Atlanta paper also survived a substantial decrease in revenue during the study period, resulting from a huge loss in circulation—including one of the most precipitous circulation drops in the entire country during the 2007 financial crisis. And the *Albany Times Union* has been trying to recover from a loss of income spurred by the erosion of its print circulation by nearly half since 2000. As at so many newspapers, the finances at these four papers mandated major cuts in the budgets available for newsgathering.

In response, all four papers cut staff over the study period, particularly since the financial crisis. At the Atlanta paper, news reports suggest, the reporting staff plummeted by about two-thirds, from about 535 in 2007 to just 180 in 2013.[3] That appears to be the largest staff cut of any of the four newspapers studied in this cohort. And at the Minneapolis paper, as of October 2013 its newsroom staff stood at 255, down by about one-third from approximately 410 in 2006.[4] *The Denver Post* has seen its newsroom staff fall by about 50 percent, from around 300 in 2006 to fewer than 200 as of 2013.[5] Much as they are reduced, those three papers still have plenty of staff left to dedicate to public affairs reporting. The challenge remains for the *Times Union*. Its reporting staff dropped from about 140 at the start of the study period to about 80 in 2015, a loss of nearly half.[6] Though that is a significant cut, the staff is still large enough to allow for some staff to be spun off onto long-term reporting projects.

One might easily assume that all these staff cuts would result in drastic decreases in the amount of original enterprise and deep accountability reporting being found by this study, as having fewer reporters would seem to imply a reduced ability to produce original reporting. Surprisingly, the medium-sized papers mostly were able to *increase* their accountability output over time. In some cases, the amount went way up. Looking at all the front-page articles in the four papers together, the 1991 sample measured 28 percent accountability. That figure jumped to 48 percent in the 2011 sample, an increase of more than 71 percent. That represents a huge shift toward original reporting in the Internet era. The amount of deep accountability reporting in the mid-sized papers also jumped during the study period, from about 2 percent of front-page content in the 1991 sample to more than 6 percent in 2011 in the four papers taken together. So despite falling resources, this group of papers somehow did *more* digging over time, not less—and they did so because editors deemed deep accountability reporting so crucial to their missions.

These figures reflect a change in attitude about what newspapers should be doing to spur readership. These metropolitan papers understand that no other news organization in their city is likely to do the amount of digging into public policy issues that they can accomplish. Not the television stations. Not the radio reporters. Not the student press. Not even the online news organizations. The data suggests that metropolitan dailies have been staking their survival on their being their communities' main provider of key information, including watchdog journalism. And in this segment of the newspaper industry, as I will show, the strategy has met with some success in terms of bringing in readers and establishing the papers' online presence.

THE *ATLANTA JOURNAL-CONSTITUTION*—MOST IMPROVED

I cannot be diplomatic about the way the *Atlanta Journal-Constitution* read in its 1991 incarnation. It was terrible. The front page was loaded with wire copy, and what articles it did produce itself were short and lacking in complexity. But the *AJC* of 2011 was so different as to be almost unrecognizable. It was loaded with both original enterprise stories on policy issues and also deep accountability stories about governmental actions. This amazing and vast transformation makes the *AJC* worthy of deeper investigation.

Given its hyphenated name, it is not surprising to learn that the *Journal-Constitution* came into being from the merger of two Atlanta newspapers.[7] The older newspaper was the *Constitution*, a morning newspaper established in 1868 when an even older paper, the *Atlanta Daily Opinion*, was purchased and renamed. *The Journal*, an afternoon paper, was founded in 1883. The newspapers hired noted writers of the times, including *Gone with the Wind* author Margaret Mitchell, who worked as a reporter for the *Journal* in the 1920s. In 1939, the *Journal* was sold to James M. Cox, a former Ohio governor and presidential candidate, who added to his media empire with the newspaper's purchase. In the 1950s, with the *Journal* pulling away in circulation and revenue, Cox purchased the *Constitution* and merged many of the two newspapers' non-editorial operations. In 1982, the two papers joined their newsrooms but put out two separate papers—a morning *Journal* and an afternoon *Constitution*. In November 2001, with the *Journal*'s circulation eroding to its lowest level in a century, the two papers officially merged under one name. For the sake of this study, I use the *Atlanta Constitution* stories for the 1991 and 1996 samples, as the *Constitution* was available for the entire study period on the available databases whereas the *Journal* was not. A combined database was available from 2001 through 2011.

Not only is the 2001 merger date relevant to this study, but so is a 2007 reorganization of the *AJC* newsroom. The move was apparently meant to consolidate operations, save money, and make the newsroom more web savvy. But it also concentrated the newspaper's infrastructure for creating accountability reporting, as was explained at the time:

> The *Journal-Constitution* this summer abolished traditional desks and reconstituted itself into four departments instead of more than a dozen. Two produce the content: News and Information, the largest department, supplies breaking news and other material directed first toward the Web. The Enterprise department develops surprising, watchdog-type stories largely for the morning newspaper.[8]

Interestingly, the paper's enterprise department was meant to focus on both simple and deep reporting, with "teams doing investigations, narratives and profiles, and explanatory journalism, along with specialists in business, sports, features and the 'kennel' of watchdogs and rovers. Their jobs demand both long-term projects and 'done-in-a-day' stories."[9] The idea was to increase readers' engagement by providing not only breaking news and lifestyle reporting on the web, but also deep local content in print. "Core print readers, research shows, particularly prize 'watchdog coverage' and 'in-depth analysis,' as well as 'community news' and 'coverage of serious issues,'" the editors reasoned. "Online readers are more apt to look for breaking news, useful information, multimedia, and interactivity."[10] Even before this reorganization, the *AJC* also required all reporters to take a training course on using the Freedom of Information Act as a way to spur more watchdog journalism.[11]

Editor Kevin Riley, who joined the *AJC* in January 2011, says that the advent of accountability reporting was also greatly spurred by audience research that began before he arrived, in 2009 or 2010, which suggested readers wanted more accountability coverage. He said the paper started compiling a "momentum score" that compared the percentage of people who thought the paper was improving overall with the percentage of those who thought it was getting worse. In July 2010, Riley says, the momentum score was -5, indicating that 5 percent more people polled thought the paper was getting worse than thought it was getting better. The score bottomed out in September 2010 at -12, according to Riley. The research prompted the paper to put more emphasis on what readers said they wanted, and that included more reporting on government. Amy Chown, the *AJC*'s vice president for marketing, wrote that the *AJC*'s research, undertaken by Cox Media Group Research and Frank N. Magid Associates, found that accountability reporting was key to attracting and keeping *AJC* readers:

> Research identified the areas that drove reader satisfaction: watchdog journalism, digging deep to tell the "real" story, and providing valuable information readers can't get elsewhere. This reader insight drove newsroom decisions and also formed the foundation of a focused marketing strategy. ... Regular topic and headline tracking studies indicated the stories readers wanted to see on their front page: strong, hard news about meaningful topics like the economy and jobs, the impact of Washington policies, the use of tax dollars, and government corruption. Readers confirmed what we had hoped: It was high-quality journalism that drove perceptions of value, not gimmicks or content we might embrace if we were chasing occasional or non-readers. Core readers demanded exactly the kind of journalism we were equipped to provide.[12]

Riley said the *Journal-Constitution* responded by making wholesale changes in what it put into the paper. "Investigative reporting and watchdog reporting became a top priority for us," he explains. "It remains in our customer's eyes based on our research the most important thing we do."[13] Riley says that since he became editor, the paper has endeavored to put some kind of accountability journalism on its front page *every single day*. He notes with pride that because of the increased focus on accountability and many other improvements, the last momentum score he had when we spoke, from March 2015, was +24—a far cry from the *AJC* he inherited.

The data gathered for this study bears out the dramatic shift in front-page content Riley describes. As Table 3–1 shows, the makeup of the *AJC* front page has changed radically during the time period studied but particularly after its research surveys. The number of total accountability stories has gone up as the overall number of front-page stories has gone down, sending the percentage of public service journalism skyrocketing in the later study years.

Over the study period, the percentage of sampled front-page stories that can be considered as representative of accountability reporting has increased more than five times, from just 11 percent in 1996 to more than 60 percent in the 2011 sample. This suggests a major realignment of the newspaper's priorities over the study period, away from wire stories and breaking news, toward original reporting—particularly original accountability stories it could highlight on its print front page and digital home page. This rise makes intuitive sense; in the Internet era, readers increasingly know the headlines before they receive their morning paper and are looking for original reports in their chosen news source to make it worth purchasing. But it took a while for the *AJC* editors to make the shift to the kind of original journalism that plays well in the digital era.

The data also suggests that more of the *AJC*'s original public affairs journalism became deeply reported rather than simple enterprise. In the 1996 sample, for instance, *all* of the coded stories were "simple enterprise" and not one had any digging. In the 2001 and 2006 samples, only about 1 percent of front-page sampled content was "deep accountability"— about the same as in 1991. But then in the 2011 sample, nearly 12 percent of the front-page articles examined were deeply reported accountability stories. This huge increase implies that management's editorial decision to

TABLE 3–1. Total Accountability Reporting (Classified as "Original Enterprise" and "Deep Accountability"), *Atlanta Journal-Constitution*, Months of April, 1991–2011

Journal-Constitution	1991	1996	2001	2006	2011	Total
Total front-page stories	167	108	188	114	76	653
Total accountability stories	27	12	27	37	46	149
Simple/Deep	25 | 2	12 | 0	25 | 2	35 | 2	37 | 9	134 | 15
% Front-page accountability	16.17%	11.11%	14.36%	32.46%	60.53%	22.82%

reorganize the newsroom in 2007 and invest more of the newspaper's resources into the production of deep, sustained watchdog reporting produced tangible results.

Not surprisingly, much of the *AJC*'s accountability reporting focused on local government—not only the city of Atlanta but also other local municipalities, including Gwinnett County, northeast of the city,[14] and DeKalb County, on the city's eastern edge.[15] The paper also investigated state government conduct,[16] aided by a veteran reporter with more than twenty years of experience covering the statehouse. The paper was particularly aggressive in watching the conduct of lawmakers, pulling disclosure reports to document their relations with lobbyists.[17] But the *Journal-Constitution* also looked at the conduct of some federal agencies, including the Food and Drug Administration, which has a strong presence in the Atlanta area.[18]

The *AJC* was not only digging into governmental actions, but also was a relatively large producer of deep public affairs reporting on nongovernmental actors. "We know we've done a lot of good investigative reporting," says Riley. "It's a high priority, and the audience has responded to it."[19] The paper's investigations delved into such subjects as high bills at private hospitals[20] and the conduct of the nongovernmental Georgia agency that accredits schools.[21] The *Journal-Constitution*'s 2011 output of investigative reporting is similar in scale to that of the business-focused *Wall Street Journal*; 3.88 percent of the *Journal*'s April 2011 front-page stories were deep investigations, much like the 3.95 percent in the *AJC*. With companies such as Delta Airlines, Home Depot, UPS, Aflac, and Coca-Cola headquartered in Georgia, there is likely no shortage of nongovernmental topics for investigation in the *Journal-Constitution*'s coverage area. [22]

What is particularly notable about the *AJC*'s change of front-page makeup and the emergence of deep reporting is that it was accomplished despite a significant downsizing of the *Atlanta Journal-Constitution* reporting staff since 2007. News reports about the *AJC* note at least two sets of major cuts at the paper around the time that the world financial crisis hit full force: a buyout in 2007 of about forty newsroom jobs[23] and a combination of voluntary and involuntary reductions of about eighty newsroom positions in 2008.[24] At the time of the second set of cuts in 2008, the newspaper's publisher warned the staff that layoffs were necessary to position the newspaper for future growth. In fact, the job cuts were part of the maneuvers that allowed the paper to return to profitability in 2010.[25]

One way the paper has been doing more with fewer people has been to increase its collaboration with other Cox properties. "You may have noticed that our journalists are working more often alongside counterparts from other Cox Media Group outlets, such as Channel 2 Action News and AM 750 and now 95.5 FM News/Talk WSB," the paper wrote in 2010. "The intent is to produce the strongest, most-comprehensive news report possible."[26] This type of consolidation of newsgathering functions by media companies seems to be increasingly common since the 2007 financial crisis. At the *AJC*, not only do reporters work more closely than before with their colleagues at other Cox properties, but many business and editorial functions were combined at Cox's four main newspapers in 2011—the *AJC*, the *Dayton Daily News*, the *Austin American-Statesman*, and the *West Palm Beach Post*.[27] This kind of money-saving arrangement may not be optimal, but in an era of tight money, it seems to help provide a way for papers to focus their limited resources on reporting. Riley says that Cox is very supportive of the *AJC*'s operations and dedicated to its long-term health. "We're profitable," he says, thanks in part to "a lot of support from the family and company that are in this business because it is meaningful to them."[28] This sentiment seems to be similar to that expressed by other editors in this newspaper cohort, who cited corporate support as a factor encouraging the creation of meaningful accountability reporting.

Nevertheless, the *Journal-Constitution* has had to deal with a significant loss of circulation. The newspaper dropped out of the top twenty-five daily American newspapers for a few years during the study period, as the *AJC* incurred some of the largest circulation losses of any American newspaper in the years following the financial crisis. During the six months ending September 20, 2009, for example, *AJC* daily circulation dropped nearly 14 percent, the largest fall among major American newspapers during that particularly dreadful auditing period.[29] Riley says that part of the drop in circulation during this time was due to the fact that the paper decided to stop delivering to far-flung parts of its delivery area where it was costing more than the subscription price to get the paper to people. He said the *AJC* was not only delivering papers in Georgia, but also to parts of Florida, Alabama, and the Carolinas. "It takes a lot of money to get a paper to Valdosta," near the Florida border, says Riley. "I'm a journalist, not a financial guy, but I do know that if your product costs more than people pay for it, it actually ends up not being good business."[30] Even discounting that change in business strategy, the *Journal-Constitution* had lost about half its readers between 2006 and 2012 as paid circulation fell from about 365,000 in 2006 to 180,000 in 2012.

Yet starting in 2013, readership again started to grow at the *AJC*, and the editors think that the improved content and increased focus on accountability reporting are the reasons why. In fact, since March 2013, the *AJC* has once again been on the list of the 25 largest U.S. dailies, with weekday circulation over 200,000 and weekends over 600,000.[31] While the week-day version of the *AJC* is still more than a third below its pre-crisis circulation, the Sunday circulation figures now exceed those from before the financial crisis. As of March 31, 2015, the Sunday *AJC* was about 13 percent above the 2006 circulation, after a massive 60 percent increase during 2013 and a healthy rise of 6 percent in 2014.

Riley says the *AJC*'s increased editorial focus on public service journalism deserves a good deal of the credit for driving the newspaper's increase in circulation. As Riley explains, "Our readers look at the paper doing serious work and being serious about it, and therefore it's something they believe in, can trust and value."[32] Other factors clearly also played a role in the *AJC*'s circulation increases, including a slight improvement in the economy, improved marketing of the *AJC*, and a lower price for the paper in its digital edition than in print. But at the same time, I find highly credible the newspaper's own conclusion that the improved content is driving circulation. The overall lesson from the twenty-year analysis of the *Atlanta Journal-Constitution* seems to be this: If a paper improves its content dramatically, readers will respond positively.

THE *MINNEAPOLIS STAR TRIBUNE*—SALVATION IN THE SUBURBS

The same basic lesson seems to be true of the next newspaper in the metropolitan cohort, the *Star Tribune* of Minneapolis. Like the Atlanta newspaper, the *Star Tribune* is the largest newspaper in its region, and one that takes its mission very seriously. "We know we are shaping the state and the region in good ways on a regular basis," says Duchesne Drew, who joined the *Star Tribune* in 1999 and served as its managing editor from 2009 to 2015.[33] He says the paper's local focus has been key to its success:

> People care about things that are happening close to home, which isn't to say that they are indifferent to things that are happening across the globe or across the country, but they care more about what's happening across the street—what's happening at city halls, what's happening at their schools, what's happening with the healthcare in their state. And the truth is there aren't enough news organizations, local news organizations, that can do a solid job of reporting those kinds of stories.[34]

Like the *AJC*, the *Star Tribune* has followed an arc over the past twenty years that has transformed the paper from a conduit of breaking news to a wide-ranging, enterprise-oriented reporting powerhouse.

And as the *Journal-Constitution* has done, the *Strib* has also re-dedicated itself in recent years to its enterprise and watchdog reporting. When editor Nancy Barnes stepped down after ten years in 2013, the paper explained, "During a time when many media companies began shifting resources away from newsgathering, [the] *Star Tribune* invested in journalism under Barnes, delivering more original local and investigative reporting."[35] The editor who replaced Barnes, Rene Sanchez, also told readers that accountability reporting was one of his priorities. "I also think we're going to push harder and harder for watchdog reporting—coverage that is truly in the public interest," he told a *Star Tribune* web chat with readers soon after taking the editorship.[36] And as at the *AJC*, the strategy to focus on meaningful original reporting seems to have reaped results in terms of both circulation and prestige in Minneapolis. The *Strib*'s high quality in recent years can be demonstrated by the fact that it won two Pulitzer Prizes in 2013, including the very prestigious award for local reporting—its first Pulitzers since 1990.

But there is one big difference between the *Star Tribune* and its metropolitan group cohort—the presence of a competing newspaper. While technically not in the same town, the *St. Paul Pioneer Press* is just a few miles away. The "*PiPress*" is another well-respected and serious newspaper, with 2014 circulation of around 240,000 on weekdays and 270,000 on Sundays.[37] Despite their physical proximity, the two Twins Cities newspapers appeal to different segments of the local population:

> To most people outside Minnesota, Minneapolis and St. Paul are the Twin Cities, as though they are conjoined. But the Mississippi River that separates the two is as much a cultural as a geographical divide. Minneapolis on the west is the corporate, urban hipster while St. Paul to the east is the solid, middle-class working stiff. In a time of tremendous pressure in the marketplace, the *Star Tribune* and the *Pioneer Press* cling to distinct identities and remain bitter competitors.[38]

In 1987, the *Star Tribune* dropped the word *Minneapolis* from its masthead and made a run at moving into *Pioneer Press* territory, with limited success. Studies show that each paper remains dominant in its city and has limited penetration in the other twin. "In 1987, publisher Roger Parkinson pegged the *Strib*'s east-metro market share versus the *St. Paul Pioneer Press* at 25 percent. A quarter-century later? A mere 32 percent," explained the independent news site MinnPost.com.[39] Still, the two newspapers share a healthy rivalry, and that would seem to be one factor propelling accountability reporting, as each paper tries to demonstrate its vitality to the area.

Another key part of the *Star Tribune*'s strategy has been to concentrate on the suburbs, particularly the ones on the Minneapolis side of the Twin Cities. The metropolitan area, after all, is home to more than 3 million people, but only about a half million live inside the city limits of Minneapolis or St. Paul. A newsroom reorganization at the *Strib* in 2007, at a time of cutbacks, was a key moment in the paper's suburban strategy.[40] Drew says the *Star Tribune* had only six suburban reporting positions before 2007, and each of those reporters had a specific topic associated with his or her beat, which limited coverage. So in the 2007 reorganization, the paper not only upped its suburban staff to twenty reporters, it gave them more freedom over what to cover. This helped the *Star Tribune* compete against other papers, says Drew—not just the *Pioneer Press*, but also suburban weeklies:

> Some beats changed. People who covered things maybe in the arts or covered really specific topical beats found themselves covering life in the north suburbs or west suburbs. And people now and then found themselves writing far more often. And so what we did was, and it was very intentional, we thought we can't afford to be swallowed by these urban weeklies that ring us, because they are doing a better job covering the bread and butter issues people care about, but we also don't want to get caught up writing about bake sales and fish frys. We want to write about stuff that matters.[41]

Drew says the *Star Tribune* was able to do a better job of engaging its readers when it rethought its content and staffing, creating accountability reporting and other types of content that mattered most to its audience.

But there was a cost—decreased national coverage. As did the *Washington Post*, the *Star Tribune* made a conscious decision to cut the number of national news stories it reported itself. Drew said that unless a national story had a significant Minnesota angle, the paper would either take its coverage from a wire service like the Associated Press or a syndication service offered by the *New York Times* or the *Washington Post*. "We're not going to try to re-create a story with our staff that is not meaningfully different than what we're going to get from the *Times* or the *Post* or the AP," Drew explains. "We want people coming to our website or picking up the paper to find stories that are interesting and/or important that they can't find anywhere else."[42] As with the *Post*, the *MST*'s strategy of cutting back on national coverage to focus more on state and local coverage resulted in more total accountability coverage and more "deep accountability" reporting in the 2011 sample than earlier—giving more credence to the idea that watchdog reporting need not die out when resource levels are limited if editors think strategically.

The data suggests not only that the amount of accountability reporting in the *Star Tribune* took off after it refocused its resources in 2007, but also that its production of public service journalism actually increased throughout the digital era. As shown in Table 3–2, the total percentage of accountability reporting found on the *Strib*'s front pages doubled between the 2001 and 2011 samples.

Both kinds of journalism on policy issues—regular enterprise and deep reporting—rose in the *Star Tribune* over time. By the 2011 sample, 41 percent of the front-page stories in the *Strib* were original enterprise stories on government or policy issues. The *Star Tribune*'s 32 percent "simple enterprise" was the highest overall of the nine papers on average, just edging out the *Washington Post*. This suggests that the two papers' similar strategy of jettisoning national reporting to focus on local coverage helped free up resources for original reports.

The *Star Tribune* also expanded its deep accountability reporting over the study period, with the single highest amount found in the 2011 sample. The deep accountability stories on government in the *Star Tribune* samples focused on state actors, with articles on such topics as the high costs of the governor's security detail[43] and major breakdowns in the state's processes for making sure teachers at public and charter schools were licensed.[44] The paper favored investigations into state issues over local ones during the months examined, as only one deep accountability story in the five-month sample focused on a local government actor—a regional development agency.[45]

Perhaps because it did not focus much on local government, the amount of deep accountability reporting in the *Star Tribune* on nongovernmental actors is much higher than in the other metropolitan dailies studied—and second in the nine newspapers sample, after the *Wall Street Journal*. The majority of *Strib* investigations in the sample focused on business issues,[46] as makes sense for a paper based in an area that is corporate headquarters for several major American companies, including Target, U.S. Bancorp,

TABLE 3–2. Total Accountability Reporting, *Minneapolis Star Tribune*, Months of April, 1991–2011

Star Tribune	1991	1996	2001	2006	2011	Total
Total front-page stories	122	87	109	105	100	523
Total accountability stories	42	33	26	40	46	187
Simple/Deep	39 | 3	32 | 1	24 | 2	36 | 4	41 | 5	172 | 15
% Front-page accountability	34.43%	37.93%	23.85%	38.10%	46.00%	35.76%

General Mills, and 3M.[47] But *Star Tribune* investigations also focused on more general public policy issues outside of business, including crime[48] and religion.[49] The *Star Tribune*'s reporting suggests that in any major city, there is no shortage of things worth investigating.

As with the Atlanta paper, the *Star Tribune*'s increasing focus on original enterprise reporting and "deep" accountability reporting seems to have won over readers in Minneapolis. Although circulation at the *Star Tribune* dipped following the 2007 financial crisis, as advertising dropped and frugal readers canceled their subscriptions, the losses in readership were not nearly as large as at many other newspapers. Circulation bottomed out in 2011, but has been growing slightly in most years since then, although 2014 circulation was still down over 15 percent on the weekday side and 6 percent on the Sunday side from 2006.[50] Still, this is far better than the numbers at many other metropolitan newspapers, and officials at the *Star Tribune* feel that their success in holding on to most of their readers is in large part due to the high quality of the reporting they offer. "People who care about state politics or regional politics—we want them to see us as the best place to learn," explains Drew. "We're not going to be the only place. Anyone who is passionate about these issues is going to go to multiple places, but we want them to start with us."[51] There are likely many reasons why readers are staying with the *Star Tribune*. But the importance of watchdog reporting would seem to be a factor adding to the paper's commercial success.

THE *DENVER POST*—FILLING THE VOID

The Denver Post is another paper that anchors its region and has staked its reputation on original reporting and deep journalism. "We take seriously our role to be a watchdog and to do probing journalism that makes a difference," explains Greg Moore, who was *The Denver Post*'s editor from 2002 to 2016.[52] "Our building sits between the statehouse and City Hall. So you need no better reminder of the responsibility to hold those in power accountable for the spending and policy decisions made by elected representatives."[53] But in other ways, *The Denver Post*'s situation during the study period is unique in that its main in-town competitor, the *Rocky Mountain News*, went out of business in February 2009. This allows for an additional facet to be added to the overall analysis of the *Post*'s commitment to watchdog reporting—the effect of losing a competing paper.

The rivalry between the *Rocky Mountain News* and *The Denver Post* had stretched back more than one hundred years, with the papers trading off the position of dominance. "Each time it seems assured one paper has won, the other ascends," explained a 1995 article about the newspapers.[54] There can be little question that the competition pushed the newspapers to achieve. Bob Burdick, who worked for both newspapers but was the president of the *Rocky* when it closed, argued that the competition drove the papers into covering important public policy issues. "Their battle, which also produced Pulitzer Prizes for The *Post* and numerous other journalistic honors, led them to compete aggressively (and not uncontroversially) in monitoring politics, development, water rights, tourism, finance, and other Western growing pains," he wrote.[55] The *Rocky Mountain News*, owned by E. W. Scripps Company from 1926 until the end of its life, and *The Denver Post*, owned by Media News since 1987, became increasingly unable to compete financially over time, as the economic situation for the media in general and in Denver in particular became tighter and tighter.

After starting to incur major losses in the 1990s, the two newspapers merged many of their non-editorial functions under a joint operating agreement (JOA) in 2001, aimed at saving the companies money while allowing them to continue to publish two papers, with separate newsgathering operations. "Newspapers in more than 25 U.S. cities have entered joint operating agreements during the past 70 years, maintaining competing newsrooms while combining such functions as advertising, circulation and printing," explained the *Seattle Post-Intelligencer* in 2003 when entering into a JOA with the rival *Seattle Times*. "The 1970 Newspaper Preservation Act legalized the deals as special exemptions to antitrust laws that ordinarily prohibit such cooperation between competitors."[56] But despite limiting costs, the *Rocky–Post* JOA wasn't enough to sustain both papers. The *Rocky* reported a loss of $16 million in 2008 alone, and the *Post*'s losses were in the same ballpark, according to media reports at the time.[57] By then, it seemed clear that Denver could support only one major daily paper. As it became clearer that one had to go, the papers' owners held negotiations for at least two years. Analysts attributed the *Post*'s survival to several factors, including a faster adaptation to the requirements of the Internet and better corporate management. The *Rocky*'s final edition was printed on February 27, 2009.

For the sake of this study, the closing of the *Rocky* as well as the signing of the JOA need to be assessed for their effect on the production of watchdog journalism at the *Post*. Therefore, the part of this book addressing *The Denver Post* will look at two specific points of time as part of its overall analysis—start of the *Rocky–Post* joint operating agreement in January 2001 and the *Rocky*'s closing in February 2009. As with other analyses, I run no regression analysis to try to isolate the effects of each event but rather try to draw logical conclusions from an analysis of the data.

Because of the *Rocky*'s demise, *The Denver Post* is one of the few American newspapers to gain large numbers of readers during the period examined by this book. The paper's weekday circulation went up by more than 60 percent from 2006 to 2011, spiking after its competitor's closing. The *Post*'s rise in circulation continued until 2014, when it had about 400,000 in print circulation during the week and around 600,000 on Sundays. The rise in *Denver Post* circulation following the closing of its main competitor suggests that the newspaper did something to attract new readers—particularly given the reticence of many loyal *Rocky* readers to switch to the *Post*. But unfortunately for the *Post*, its total print circulation has dropped since the study period ended, to 135,000 copies weekdays and 250,000 copies on Sundays as of mid-2016, although it reportedly continues to enjoy double-digit growth each year in its digital readership.[58]

And at the same time that circulation was growing at *The Denver Post* before and after the *Rocky*'s demise, staff numbers were falling. Staff size at the *Post* dropped by half from 2006 to 2015, from about 300 to 145.[59] And the layoffs were a matter of not just quantity, but also of quality. Some of its most lauded staff members were let go, as were the majority of its copy editors. In 2011, for instance, blogger Michael Roberts documented how the *Post* arranged "buyouts of Pulitzer Prize–winning cartoonist Mike Keefe and eighteen others late last year, the March layoffs of columnists Mike Littwin and Penny Parker, among others, and farewells for two-thirds of the paper's copy editors, expected to be out by month's end."[60] Roberts's list of those laid off or taking buyouts included one staffer who had been at the *Post* for 45 years and another who had been there 44 years.[61] The reduction in staff coupled with extreme financial pressure would seem to be factors that might discourage the production of original enterprise reporting and deep investigative journalism at *The Denver Post* of 2011. However, the data suggests a different story.

A SILVER LINING?

Over the study period, *The Denver Post* actually drastically increased its commitment to original reporting on public affairs topics, like the *Journal-Constitution* and the *Star Tribune*. Looking at Table 3–3, one can see that the total percentage of accountability reporting more than doubled at the *Post* between 1991 and 2011.

Generally higher and higher numbers of accountability reports were being produced over the study years, even as the total number of front-page stories dropped, raising the overall percentage of accountability reporting. This suggests a swing away from breaking news and toward

TABLE 3–3. Total Accountability Reporting, *Denver Post*, Months of April, 1991–2011

Denver Post	1991	1996	2001	2006	2011	Total
Total front-page stories	90	103	111	98	78	480
Total accountability stories	21	28	34	32	38	153
Simple/Deep	21 | 0	23 | 5	32 | 2	29 | 3	34 | 4	139 | 14
% Front-page accountability	23.33%	27.18%	30.63%	32.65%	48.72%	31.88%

original reporting over time despite financial pressures, consistent with the results at other metropolitan newspapers.

What stands out about these results is the increase in public affairs–reporting figures at the *Post* after the *Rocky Mountain News* went under in 2009. Accountability reporting jumped 50 percent overall from 2006 to 2011 in the *Post* sample. Furthermore, "deep accountability" increased from about 3 to 5 percent of front-page stories from 2006 to 2011, an increase of two-thirds. These figures suggest that the demise of its competitor liberated *The Denver Post* to do the kind of original accountability reporting it really wanted to do, without having to concentrate on matching the *Rocky* on breaking news. As editor Moore explains:

> We have felt an enormous responsibility to do serious watchdog reporting and to just generally dig harder. Losing the *Rocky* took a couple hundred journalists off the case here so people expect even more from the *Post*. It surely has helped us to be more free to focus on what we think is important as opposed to worrying about matching whatever we thought the *Rocky* was doing. I think both papers spent a lot of resources matching one another.[62]

Conventional wisdom in the news business is that losing a paper creates less news for consumers overall, and this is certainly true. But the creation of more original accountability reporting by the surviving paper represents a small "silver lining." The data also shows a small rise in the amount of accountability stories in the 2001 sample, taken just after the *Post* and the *Rocky* had entered their joint operating agreement.

An examination of the *Post*'s deep watchdog reporting shows considerable resources going into examinations of government action, albeit to varying degrees over time. The percentage of deeply reported front-page accountability stories in the *Post* about governmental actors varied over the study period from 0 in the 1991 sample to more than 5 percent in the 2011 sample. The *Post*'s 2011 figures are particularly impressive. In that year, more than 5 percent of front-page stories were deep watchdog stories, reflecting the newspaper's substantial commitment to keeping government accountable. As is to be expected, the deep watchdog reporting in the *Post* focused mainly on local issues. Out of thirteen total watchdog stories in the twenty-year sample, eight of the articles focused on city or county issues. There was particular emphasis on the conduct of Denver-area police and firefighters, who were the subject of four of the eight local "deep watchdog" articles. Three of the watchdog stories involved state government, which makes sense given that Denver is the Colorado state capital. And one "deep watchdog" story was about a federal agency, the Department of Energy, and its work at the Rocky Flats nuclear weapons production facility outside Denver.[63]

However, the *Post* did few deep accountability stories about nongovernmental actors. The sample suggests the paper may be underproducing accountability stories on NGOs, institutes, or companies, as many of them are based in the Denver area, including Dish Network, Coors Brewing, and investment powerhouse Janus Group.[64] If editors are choosing to direct deep reporting into watchdog stories, that would be understandable given the extensive resources required for investigations and Denver's status as a state capital.

That said, the *Post* seems committed to accountability reporting even in the wake of Moore's resignation in mid-2016. The new editor, Lee Ann Colacioppo, has divided the newsroom of about one hundred people into a "Now" team that will focus on breaking news and an "Enterprise" team that will focus on more deeply reported stories. The Enterprise team will do "the kind of work that makes newspapers newspapers," Colacioppo told *Editor & Publisher*, meaning public policy and investigative work.[65] While this study suggests that the *Post* is embracing its role as a watchdog over the government, recent press reports about continuing resource issues at the paper suggest it will need to concentrate its efforts like never before to keep up its commitment to public service journalism.

THE *ALBANY TIMES UNION*—STAKING IT ALL ON THE STATE

The three metropolitan dailies studied so far in this chapter have all made accountability reporting an increasingly important part of their output, raising the amount of both "simple enterprise" and "deep accountability" stories over time. The story of the fourth paper in this group, the *Albany Times Union*, provides somewhat of a contrast. On the one hand, the *Times Union* has also staked its success on being a vibrant watchdog, focusing its efforts on New York state government. "There's the mission-driven responsibility to do watchdog reporting because if we don't, nobody will, and we owe it to our community to do that," says Rex Smith, editor of the *Times Union*.[66] The paper attracts thousands of readers who count on its coverage of the halls of power in Albany. Also, as the smallest paper in this segment, the *ATU* has had the greatest difficulty keeping its accountability reporting levels high over time. As budgets have tightened, leading to staff cuts, the Albany paper has struggled to keep its accountability reporting levels steady. The amount of public affairs journalism varied considerably from sample to sample, and the paper never again captured in the later study years the very high level of accountability reporting done in its 1991 sample. The *ATU* continues to have very high aspirations when it comes to producing accountability reporting, to be sure, and the editors manage to deliver relatively large amounts of public service journalism even as economic pressures have mounted. But a study of the *Albany Times Union* suggests that accountability journalism is sensitive to budgets and resource levels, even when the editors try to keep its output high. This would seem to be bad news for smaller newspapers, where editors have the fewest resources available to enable public service journalism to flow.

The *Times Union*'s position as the major news source in New York state's capital has been central to its success—driving readership as well as giving *ATU* staff an important focus for their reporting efforts. "When it comes to taking a deep look at state government and how it operates and generating enterprise, we really believe that we're the ones that have to do that," explains Smith.[67] Smith also says that spending on investigations and deep watchdog reporting is a good business move:

> My newspaper is in its 160th year right now—founded 1856, so we're past the 160 mark—and it's not going to survive another 160 based on full run print advertising, nor I don't think on banner ads on home pages. It [the *Times Union*'s future] really is going to have to be based on the value proposition that we give people who invest time with us the kind of content that they just can't find elsewhere.[68]

Indeed, a glance at the paper shows that stories about state government are plentiful, as are articles on local government. More than 40 percent of the accountability stories examined in the *ATU* over the study period focused on state and local government, dwarfing any other single topic. Still, the newspaper has struggled to keep its overall levels of watchdog reporting steady despite having two major advantages: strong corporate support for its mission, and a well-composed online strategy.

The *Times Union*'s owners have always been willing to invest in good content. The newspaper traces its history to 1856, when it was a four-page broadsheet, published under the motto "Independence now, independence forever."[69] It was risky to open a newspaper in a city of 50,000 people already oversaturated with dailies—it had five at the time—but the owners of the Albany *Morning Times* thought there was room for a nonpartisan newspaper in the sea of partisan press. And the paper has a long tradition of putting accountability journalism at its core. By the turn of the twentieth century, by which time the paper had acquired its current name, "the *Times Union* began to take its role as a standard bearer of the Fourth Estate with a sense of mission."[70] With that strategy, the *Times Union* thrived even as many of its competitors went under. Only a small family-owned paper in adjacent Schenectady remains in greater Albany today.

The *Times Union* grew even stronger after being acquired by media baron William Randolph Hearst in 1924. Hearst was on a buying spree during those years, building a newspaper empire that has grown to be a $10 billion-a-year diversified media company.[71] Being part of a large company gave the *Times Union* new opportunities. "With market leadership and Hearst's deep pockets, the *Times Union* enjoyed decades of prosperity."[72] As of late 2017, George R. Hearst III, a member of the founding family, was still serving as the *Albany Times Union*'s publisher—making it the only Hearst property being run by a direct descendant of William Randolph Hearst, according to Smith.

Smith, who has been with the *Times Union* since 1995, says the company does much to enrich the paper's ability to serve as a check on the government. First of all, he says his supportive publisher stands behind the paper, even when the *Times Union* writes critical articles about personal friends of his. Second, Smith says the *ATU* gets lots of support from the Hearst Corporation's top management. For instance, in the early 2000s, Smith says, the current head of the corporation, Steven R. Swartz—then a senior executive—told the largest five Hearst dailies to go out and raid their competition for the best investigative journalists. Swartz said Hearst would pay their salaries for the first year to signify how important accountability reporting was to the company. This allowed Smith to hire people he wouldn't have gotten otherwise. "That was a signifier, really, of the commitment at the top level of then the newspaper division, now of the corporation, to this kind of journalism," he says.[73] Another way that Smith says the corporation encourages watchdog reporting is to fund lawsuits against government entities that are trying to stand in the way of open reporting—and let the newspapers involved keep any cash judgments that result. Smith says this helps lift the morale of the entire newsroom and encourages the production of even more watchdog reporting, because the proceeds can be plowed into new investigative projects.

But how has that corporate commitment affected the paper's bottom line? It is hard to say, because Hearst is a privately held company and therefore not required to file public financial statements. This makes it difficult to garner much information about *the Albany Times Union's* profitability—but there can be no question that both paid circulation and staff sized dipped over the length of the study. Back in 1985, the *Times Union* had circulation of 101,000 daily and 160,000 on Sunday and had 146 employees in the newsroom.[74] Circulation apparently held steady through the early 2000s, as the paper weathered some turbulent economic times:

> The *Times Union* experienced a significant downturn, but it never lost money, and it remained one of the most financially successful of the Hearst papers. From the outside, it looked in 2004 as if the paper had emerged from the economic turmoil largely unscathed and with most of its staff— 269 employees, 137 in the newsroom—intact.[75]

But later in the decade, after the world financial crisis hit, the *Times Union* seemed to finally feel the pinch—shedding readers and reporting staff. By March 2013, its print circulation had fallen to 66,000 on weekdays. By March 2014, circulation was lower still: 55,000 on weekdays and 62,000 on Sundays.[76] That would seem to indicate a fall in print ad revenue similar to what we have seen with other daily newspapers analyzed for this book. But those figures alone do not tell the full story because of the *Times Union's* vibrant online presence.

Another characteristic that sets the *Times Union* apart from other papers in this segment of the study is that it was a very early adapter of a strong online culture. After setting up its first website in August 1996, the *ATU* was relatively quick to see the ways in which online news could become an asset:

> Most newspapers its size had little more on their websites than a community bulletin board and classified advertising modified for the Web. But the *Times Union* went further, emulating larger and richer papers such as the *Washington Post* in offering extensive archives, dedicated online teams, and links to reporters' email addresses.[77]

As the newspaper started to examine its production processes to see how they could be adapted for the web, it hired a consultant, who found that it took more than 213 steps to get a story on the web or into print. This process clearly needed to be streamlined if the paper were to post news around-the-clock in a timely manner. The newsroom had to become a "nimble, efficient and responsive operation that embraces and employs multimedia newsgathering techniques in order to meet the demand for customized news and information 24 hours a day, seven days a week, on multiple platforms."[78] The larger goal, says Smith, was to be able to redeploy resources then being used to create web content separately from print content into one unified news operation, to enable more public service journalism. "We needed to look at how we produced stuff so that we could be more efficient, and supposedly the theory was that [that] would enable us to continue to have the resources to do the deeper reporting," he explains.[79] In other words, the paper had to become more efficient to do the kinds of reporting it most aspired to do.

To that end, the *Times Union* launched a formal project in 2006 codenamed Prometheus, for the Greek hero who enables progress, to transform its newsroom—and business model—into one for the Internet era. The project focused specifically on the creation of original enterprise journalism:

> News had to get on the Web quickly, and it needed to be accurate. But stories also had to be smarter. The *Times Union* needed an organizational structure that freed up time so reporters could focus on writing stories that gave the paper's audiences more than they could get elsewhere. Stories that provided context, local flavor and interpretation—plus a vivid multimedia presentation for the online version—would hopefully reward loyal readers and attract new ones. Increased readership would bring back advertisers, creating a virtuous circle.[80]

For its time, the project was revolutionary, particularly coming from such a small outlet. "No newspaper had attempted to map and overhaul a newsroom in the way the *Times Union* was contemplating."[81] Smith says the project was a "partial success," because the new site came online just before the recession, which caused some of the changes to be sidelined. But Smith says the most important legacy from the project is that everyone at the *ATU* produces material for both print and web at once, which helps the paper maintain the resources to do deep reporting projects. Smith says having everyone produce multiple types of content is now the practice at the other Hearst newspapers, as well as throughout the industry. This was not the setup at most newspapers early in the digital era, which typically had a print staff and separate web staff. The 2006 start date of the Prometheus project therefore provides another key date for evaluating the *ATU*'s output of accountability reporting, for insight into how a newspaper's approach to online news production affects the content.

The *ATU*'s Prometheus project has also brought it good results in terms of driving digital traffic. Figures are not available for the study period, but post-study data suggests geometric growth in online readership. As of June

2014, timesunion.com was receiving more than 20 million page views per month from more than 235,000 discrete viewers.[82] By the summer of 2015, the *ATU*'s web traffic had nearly doubled again, to 35 million page views per month, according to Smith. That is many times the number of print subscribers, and many times the web traffic generated by the other newspapers in this cohort. Although there was no paywall on the *ATU* site or on any of the Hearst newspaper sites during the study period, the paper did add one in January 2016. Previous to that, web traffic contributed to the *Times Union*'s paper's bottom line by driving up digital ad rates. The addition of a paywall for the *ATU*'s best content suggests that the strategy of trying to rely on online ads for income just did not bring in enough revenue overall.

PROMETHEUS TURNS THE TIDE

Still, the data suggests that the Prometheus project did boost the *Times Union*'s flagging production of public service journalism. The paper had cycled up and down in the overall production of accountability journalism during the study period, but unlike almost every other paper examined, it was far stronger in 1991 than in later years. The trend has generally gone the opposite way in the papers studied for this book—particularly in the other medium-sized newspapers. In the 1991 *Times Union* sample, more than half of the paper's front-page content consisted of some kind of accountability reporting. But as shown in Table 3–4, there was considerable drop-off during certain years. In the 1996 sample, for instance, the percentage of front-page accountability stories fell by more than half from the previous one. The 2006 sample had less still, when only about one-fifth of the front-page content was enterprise stories dealing in some way with public policy issues. But that changed after Prometheus.

That the lowest percentage of original accountability reports in the study was found in the 2006 sample suggests that the staff's efforts were stretched particularly thin by the pre-Prometheus demands of the Internet, when they were producing print and web content separately. The

TABLE 3–4. Total Accountability Reporting, *Albany Times Union*, Months of April, 1991–2011

Albany Times Union	1991	1996	2001	2006	2011	Total
Total front-page stories	63	82	87	97	83	412
Total accountability stories	34	20	28	21	33	136
Simple/Deep	30 | 4	19 | 1	25 | 3	17 | 4	30 | 3	121 | 15
% Front-page accountability	53.97%	24.39%	32.18%	21.65%	39.76%	33.01%

increase in the percentage of accountability reporting after Project Prometheus was implemented—an 83 percent jump in accountability reports from 2006 levels in the 2011 sample—suggests that the changes the *Times Union* made in its news production process did lead to the production of more accountability journalism, precisely as its editors had hoped. Those changes helped the *ATU* turn around the slide in total public service reporting it had seen in the samples between 1996 and 2006. Thanks in part to the boost in accountability in the final sample, as well as its strong start, the *Times Union* ended up being third of nine papers overall in the total percent of accountability found on its sampled front pages, surpassed only by the *Washington Post* and the *Wall Street Journal*. This means that in terms of total accountability reporting, the *ATU* surpassed not only all the small and medium-sized dailies studied, but the *New York Times* as well. That speaks to the *ATU*'s deep commitment to covering state government in New York, despite the challenges it faced in terms of available resources.

The data also confirms the *Times Union*'s abiding interest in deep watchdog reporting. Each sample had three or four "deep watchdog" reports—about one per week—except for 1996, when there was just one during the entire month examined. The *ATU*'s overall rate, 3.64 percent front-page "deep accountability," was surpassed in the study only by the *Washington Post* and the *Wall Street Journal*. And if we exclude the "deep accountability" reports involving nongovernmental actors, the *Albany Times Union* scored second of the nine papers in terms of highest percentage of deep reporting on government, behind the *Washington Post*. These are not results I would have expected going into the study. The results suggest that in streamlining and improving its newsgathering for the digital era, the *Times Union* also created mechanisms to enhance not only the creation of simple enterprise reporting on policy and government, but also the kind of deep reporting that is difficult and costly to accomplish. There would seem to be a lesson here for other newspapers: Resources saved by making newsgathering more efficient can be redeployed toward the creation of important original reporting.

Much of the *ATU*'s watchdog reporting focused on the behavior of state employees, be they legislators[83] or bureaucrats.[84] This reporting was often made possible by Freedom of Information Act requests[85] or by leaks of documents or videos.[86] The paper also spent considerable resources to research some of its stories, paying for an independent study to examine state lottery advertising[87] or spending months combing through computerized state records for a series on tainted public water supplies.[88] Wrongdoing by police was a favorite topic for the *ATU*'s locally focused reporting during the five sample months examined.[89]

Although the *Times Union* staff has been downsized, Smith said his team manages somehow to continue to dig out important accountability stories. He explains that he is constantly balancing how many resources the paper will devote to "generating the clickable stuff" and how much it can invest in "the kind of accountability reporting that meets your mission and sets apart your brand."[90] Journalism is a team effort, after all, and the data presented here suggests that the entire *Times Union* team is succeeding in creating meaningful public service journalism despite the considerable difficulties in balancing out competing needs—or at least it was during the years studied. As Smith, who reviewed the study's results before speaking with me, concluded, "I like reading your piece, because it suggests that maybe we're hitting the sweet spot."[91] But I would need to review the data for years after 2011 to make sure that the *ATU* continued to keep its creation of accountability reporting at high levels. The addition of a paywall suggests that the paper is working harder than ever to create an auspicious financial footing for continued public service journalism.

CONCLUSIONS: TWO PATHWAYS AHEAD

The data collected for this part of the study offers substantial evidence that accountability reporting is being produced in spades at some representative metropolitan dailies. Although not every paper studied increased its accountability output steadily from year to year, there was an upward trend overall, as the papers strengthened the watchdog role they play for their communities. For three of the newspapers, this led to substantial changes in front-page content over the study years. Rather than focus on breaking news and, in some cases, relying on wire copy, the Atlanta, Minneapolis, and Denver papers have produced high amounts of original reporting on public policy issues and extremely respectable amounts of deep accountability reporting. The fourth paper, the *Albany Times Union*, also created relatively high amounts of public service journalism and sees doing so as central to its mission, but it has stepped back somewhat from the levels of accountability reporting it achieved early in the study. The *Times Union* has also had to work increasingly hard to keep its accountability work at high levels, as its staff and resource levels have fallen, and seems to have come across only more challenges since the study period ended in 2011. This seems to suggest that medium-sized newspapers have to make choices—often tough choices—about where to deploy their limited resources to create the kind of watchdog reporting they aspire to offer their readers.

The Atlanta and Albany papers make a particularly interesting pair for a comparison, having followed quite different paths over the past twenty years. The *Atlanta Journal-Constitution* came to the accountability game quite late, but it jumped in with both feet when it did. Since this book was written, the *AJC* has not only kept up the pace by striving to have an original accountability story on its front page every day, but it has also dedicated considerable resources to developing its capability to do investigative journalism. This approach has not only brought the *Journal-Constitution* national attention, but it has benefited the newspaper's bottom line, through increased subscriptions and the kind of growing digital traffic that the paper can monetize.

The *Albany Times Union*, on the other hand, just seems to be stretched thinner and thinner. Although it still remains steadfastly dedicated to its role as the chief watchdog over New York state government, the paper seems to be burdened by the weight of having to do everything well that it needs to do well in order to succeed in the digital era. Other indicators gathered by the study suggest that the *ATU* has become less deep in its reporting over time: Both average article length and average number of sources per accountability article fell to the lowest point for the *ATU* in the 2011 sample,[92] and the complexity of the topics covered also moved that year away from systemic problems and more toward issues involving just a few wrongdoers.[93] The paper also seems to be more focused than ever on bringing in revenue. Today, sponsored content seems to dominate its web pages. There are many slideshows available and other content that requires lots of "clicks" to get through, boosting the newspaper's digital usage. The good journalism is still there, like a multipart 2016 series about the legacy of the heavily polluted "Superfund" sites left in the Albany region.[94] However, the *Times Union* articles in that series are behind a paywall, available only to subscribers or those who sign up for paid digital access.[95] Much as some readers would like to read these stories for free, I can certainly understand why the *ATU* is insisting people pay to read its best content. This monetization strategy suggests that keeping the *Times Union*'s web pages free of charge and raising its digital ad rates to account for high online readership just did not bring in as much revenue as hoped. This fits with the larger strategy of using accountability reporting to induce people not just to *read* a newspaper, but *pay for* a newspaper. I suppose it is far better for a newspaper to charge for accountability journalism in order to fund it rather than cut back on that most important kind of reporting. But putting accountability content behind a paywall also limits community access.

The differences between the *Journal-Constitution* and the *Times Union* also speak to how newspapers can use accountability reporting to define themselves in the digital marketplace and capitalize on the competitive advantages they have over other news organizations. The *Journal-Constitution* could probably get away with doing very little public service journalism and still have people buy the paper, because it is the main news source for the bustling city of Atlanta. Yet interestingly, its management has chosen to make accountability its centerpiece. Many people will buy the *AJC* for things like cultural and business coverage, but the one thing—in fact, the *only* thing—getting the paper national attention is its award-quality investigations. While I doubt this strategy is going to turn the *Journal-Constitution* into a national paper, it could help transform it into the South's dominant newspaper. The *Times Union*, on the other hand, really has little choice but to be a watchdog over New York state government, as its comparative advantage is in being the single best source of news in a very important state capital. That's the card it has played for decades, and really the card it must continue to play successfully in a digital world to keep the paper on sound financial ground—especially as it faces increasing competition from online news organizations like Politico.

All four newspapers studied in this chapter face local competition from online news organizations as well as broadcasters, but the competition is particularly acute in Minneapolis. "We feel pressure from every direction on the dial. We feel pressure from Minnesota Public Radio and all the other places people can go for information," says Drew of the *Star Tribune*. In Minneapolis, for instance, one of the places news consumers can go is to MinnPost.com. Founded in 2007 by a former editor and publisher of the *Star Tribune*, MinnPost calls itself a "nonprofit, nonpartisan enterprise whose mission is to provide high-quality journalism for people who care about Minnesota."[96] With a full-time staff of about fifteen and part-time staff of over forty contributors, MinnPost posts several stories a day, from news to culture to sports. Now reportedly making a profit, the site is one of the most successful municipal news sites in the United States and "a significant player in an educated, news hungry Twin Cities market."[97] The other cities in the metropolitan group are home to multiple sites dedicated to news and policy issues, but they currently lack a high-quality online news organization as strong as MinnPost's. The existence of some other excellent city-focused digital news organizations suggests that metropolitan newspapers must focus on engaging their readers with civic journalism, or someone else will. This just adds to the financial pressure on America's metropolitan papers—as if they needed any more. But so far, newspapers are still proving that they are the highest producers of watchdog journalism—and these mid-sized papers show just how much a strategy focused on accountability reporting can help them navigate the choppy waters in which American journalism finds itself today.

The issue of finances will be central to the next chapter of this book, where I discuss accountability journalism at small local newspapers. As Chapter 4 will demonstrate, the accountability journalism situation is much less uniform among small newspapers, some of which, but not all, are working overtime to produce deep watchdog journalism. Given that small dailies like the ones to be studied in the next chapter make up the bulk of American newspapers, their lack of widespread, deep accountability reporting is problematic. In contrast to the medium-sized cities studied, small American communities may be missing out on a newspaper that is fully focused on its watchdog role.

CHAPTER 4

America's Most Vulnerable

America's small newspapers have been feeling the pinch in recent years, as falling readership has translated into smaller budgets. There's little doubt in the industry that public service journalism has been affected. Veteran journalists like former *Oregonian* editor Sandy Rowe say that many small news organizations have had to cut back on their enterprise and watchdog reporting in response to fiscal realities, harming their ability to play the watchdog role. "Local and regional journalism do not produce enough accountability reporting to fully engage and empower citizens, jeopardizing their ability to hold government, business and civic leaders accountable," she wrote.[1] The U.S. government also seems to agree that there is too little accountability reporting on the local level. A 2011 Federal Communication Commission report on *The Information Needs of Communities* expressed deep concern over the implications of too little public service journalism at small newspapers:

> This is likely to lead to the kinds of problems that are, not surprisingly, associated with a lack of accountability—more government waste, more local corruption, less effective schools, and other serious community problems. The independent watchdog function that the Founding Fathers envisioned for journalism—going so far as to call it crucial to a healthy democracy—is in some cases at risk at the local level.[2]

You might think the U.S. government would want *less* scrutiny from the press, not more. Yet even many of the public officials subject to the press's watchful eye understand well the long-term importance to our democracy of meaningful accountability reporting.

Editors of small newspapers also understand the crucial role that accountability journalism plays in their communities. "Watchdog reporting is what we're about," says Joan Krauter, executive editor of one of the newspapers discussed in this chapter, the *Bradenton* (Florida) *Herald*.[3] Doug Bauer, managing editor of the other newspaper studied in depth, the *Lewiston* (Idaho) *Tribune*, says small newspapers like his bring veracity into the digital world. "People trust our brand," he says. "They know if we're reporting something, that we stand by it—that we've done our due diligence."[4] These editors of small papers know that if their news organizations don't put a spotlight on government malfeasance, it is unlikely that anyone else will. The news ecosystems are so small in their towns that the local newspaper is usually the main source of information and certainly the news organization most likely to dig deeply into accountability issues.

This chapter's portrait of this final segment of the American newspaper industry—the small newspapers—will suggest that although these papers take seriously their responsibility to police the work of government and industry, their size and strength do affect what they are able to achieve. These two newspapers—one small, and one very small—show that local papers *are* able to produce accountability reporting and even some deeply reported watchdog stories, despite their limited size. But the depth of the paper's resources seems to relate directly to the quantity and quality of their accountability output. The larger of the two papers, the *Bradenton Herald,* churned out a relatively small but extremely steady flow of accountability journalism in the months studied, including deeply reported stories. But the other small paper examined, the very small *Lewiston Tribune*, did far less accountability journalism overall than the *Herald*. More notably, it did almost no sustained digging in the stories examined over the twenty-year horizon. Moreover, neither of the papers studied in this group produced any deep investigations of nongovernmental actors at all during the five study months. These results are not to imply that these two newspapers do no deep investigatory reporting at all, for they certainly do—nor to imply that the *Lewiston Tribune* never does any deep accountability reporting, for it certainly does. However, the lack of such stories in the months studied suggests a wider deficit.

These results suggest that even when they have high aspirations, small newspapers are limited in the amount of accountability reporting they can produce by their low resource levels. This is problematic, as so many newspapers in the United States fall into this category. Approximately 7,500 daily and weekly newspapers in America have a circulation of 30,000 or fewer.[5] As I drove from California to New York during the summer of 2016, I purchased copies of all the small newspapers I could find, including ones whose titles are not household names, like the *Del Norte* (California) *Triplicate*, the *Lovelock* (Nevada) *Review-Miner*, and the *Traverse City* (Michigan) *Record-Eagle*. Small newspapers like these dot the country and are often the only press around to monitor local governments. The results of my research into small papers also suggest that given their relatively small staffs and tight budgets, when these sorts of papers have resources left after they cover news to undertake deep reporting, they are choosing to focus on the work of the government to fulfill the watchdog role, rather than on the work of nongovernmental actors. This makes sense, given the wide acceptance of the watchdog role as a core function of newspapers. But this leaves all kinds of important local nongovernmental actors that play a role in public policy without proper scrutiny. It is critically important that America's smaller papers continue to shine a light on public policy issues and keep a watchful eye out for all kinds of misdeeds, as they are on the front lines of accountability for their communities.

STRUGGLING TO "DO IT ALL"

The *Bradenton Herald* and the *Lewiston Tribune* were chosen for study as representatives of the small-paper segment for several reasons. First, when the study began, they were two of the only small newspapers in the United States that were available going all the way back to 1991 in electronic databases. They also represent geographic diversity, as they are located in two different parts of the country—the Southeast and the Northwest. The two small papers also represent different ownership structures. The *Bradenton Herald* is owned by the McClatchy newspaper chain, which currently owns more than two dozen daily and weekly papers.[6] The smaller *Lewiston Tribune* is independent, with majority ownership by the family that founded the paper more than 120 years ago.[7] The papers also represent slightly different size profiles. The *Bradenton Herald* had a 2015 circulation of 31,000 on weekdays and 45,000 on Sundays.[8] The *Lewiston Tribune* is about half as large, with a 2015 circulation of 20,000 on weekdays and 22,000 on Sundays.[9] The difference in size translates to differing resource levels, and that affects the production of public affairs journalism. The *Herald* and the *Tribune* are different enough to suggest some generalizations about watchdog journalism at local newspapers. These conclusions come after I examined 790 front-page stories at the two small papers—476 at the *Bradenton Herald* and 314 articles at the *Lewiston Tribune.*

The takeaway from this study of the small-newspaper segment suggests that they continue to struggle to do everything well in the digital era. Not only do local papers still need to get out their print editions, but their teams of journalists also need 24/7 newsgathering operations active on both the web and on social media. They need to shoot videos, do podcasts, and produce photo slide shows. Over the study period, they have had to do more tasks over time with fewer staff. Every newspaper in America faces the same issues, but the challenges are acute for these small newspapers, spread thinner and thinner over time. At the newspapers studied, the effects of the stretching of resources on the accountability journalism being produced are quite visible.

One way to see the stress manifesting itself is by looking at the amount of "simple enterprise" stories on these small papers' front pages. Unlike most of the other newspapers studied for this book, there was *less* original public service journalism on the front pages of the two small newspapers after the 1996 sample, not more. While the Internet freed larger newspapers from having to focus on breaking news, sending the amount of original enterprise reporting they did skyward, its advent did not have the same effect for small local papers. The small papers did less original accountability reporting as the Internet became a larger factor in American life, likely because they did not have the ability to shift resources into producing original enterprise reports, as the larger papers did. A newspaper that sees its staff fall from, say, 250 to 150 reporters still has enough journalists to keep accountability reporting flowing at a steady clip. But at a small paper, it is hard to put anyone on accountability reporting projects at all if you have, say, just 30 reporters total and they are busy keeping up with a digital world. A cut to 25 journalists makes it even harder.

Much as their editors realize the importance of accountability reporting, these small newspapers remain a main source of information for their communities, and must produce large quantities of hard news. The collected data suggests that is where the small papers studied dedicate much of their resources. This is a different situation from the one faced by the larger newspapers studied. For instance, readers in Minneapolis are able to get breaking local news from not only two major dailies, but also from a number of online news sites, weekly papers, local television stations, and Minnesota Public Radio. On the other hand, in Lewiston, besides the *Tribune* there is only one local television station and some lightly staffed radio stations to report breaking local news. The lack of a larger news ecosphere in many small cities and towns means that breaking news, not enterprise reporting, is still at the heart of many small local news operations, even in the Internet era.

This study identified other indicators of the stress that the Bradenton and Lewiston papers feel as they try to be vibrant watchdogs in the digital era, including an increased reliance on government sources overall and a sharp fall in the number of outside experts being quoted in stories. The complexity of these papers' accountability journalism has also generally fallen over time, particularly between 2006 and 2011, as staff size dropped.[10] At the same time, these two small newspapers have both managed to keep average story length and number of sources quoted per story relatively constant over time, despite reductions in resource levels. As we will see in the detailed discussion of each paper, these small newspapers continue to value public affairs reporting highly, despite the considerable challenges they face in producing it.

BRADENTON HERALD—A BITE OUT OF METRO TAMPA

The west coast of Florida is not only crowded with residents—some 4 million in the greater Tampa region[11]—but also awash in newspapers. Like much of Florida, the area consists heavily of retirees, and they still consume newspapers in relatively high numbers.[12] Greater Tampa's news-loving population had been supporting four daily newspapers during the twenty years that are the focus of this study—papers fighting among themselves for readers and advertising dollars. One of those papers succumbed in 2016, when the *Tampa Tribune* was purchased by its bigger rival, the *Tampa Bay Times*, and then closed.[13] Although the closure of the *Tribune* happened after the end of my study period, it illustrates the tightness in the market that the *Bradenton Herald* and other Tampa-area papers were feeling at the time and still feel today, despite their being among a populace that still loves getting a print paper on the doorstep every morning.

There can be little doubt that the *Tampa Bay Times*—which was known as the *St. Petersburg Times* until 2012—has been the king of the local hill. Not only is it Florida's highest-circulation daily[14]—larger in circulation than the *Miami Herald*—but it is also a particularly well-respected newspaper because of its ownership by a journalism nonprofit, the Poynter Institute. The *Times* has won twelve Pulitzer Prizes since 1898, including five during the twenty years studied. The *Tampa Tribune*—located just across Old Tampa Bay—was ground down and eventually put out of business after decades of head-to-head competition with the *Times*. The presence of multiple competitors in the area has made it necessary for the two smaller local papers in the region, the *Bradenton Herald* and the *Sarasota*

Herald-Tribune,[15] to focus on the unique roles they play in their towns to help define and keep their audiences.

The *Bradenton Herald* is hardly a niche paper. It serves a city of more than 50,000 people,[16] located in a fast-growing county south of Tampa, with more than 350,000 residents.[17] But with three other dailies nearby during the years studied, the *Herald* has had to be *the* authoritative source for information in its hometown and its home county, Manatee, to find an audience. "What happens in St. Pete and Tampa doesn't always translate here," explains *Bradenton Herald* editor Joan Krauter. "A great day is when all five or six stories on the [*Herald*] front page are local, and that's more days out of the week than not."[18] Krauter says she considers the *Herald-Tribune* in Sarasota, south of Bradenton, a direct competitor and worries less about the Tampa papers. The *Herald* also has had an in-town online competitor, the *Bradenton Times*, since 2012—although the site posts far less material every day than the newspaper does.[19] The *Herald* says the digital audience for its own website, www.bradenton.com, is growing by double digits yearly. It had an average of 3.7 million page views monthly with more than 800,000 discrete visitors per month as of June 2014, and 4.2 million page views monthly with 1.5 million unique visitors by mid-2017.[20] The paper instituted a paywall after the study period ended and keeps experimenting with its price and placement. Its large digital footprint and relatively high local readership suggest that the *Herald* is the most comprehensive source of news in its hometown.

For the *Herald*, giving readers not only hard news but also accountability reporting about Bradenton has been key to its survival in a crowded market. "It's our responsibility to hold the government officials accountable. And nobody else is going to do it," Krauter explains.[21] She says that one way the paper is able to encourage the production of deep accountability reporting is to build it into reporters' annual goals. She says *Herald* staff members are asked to "pick what topic you want to dive into. Then we find time to let the reporter work on that issue or issues."[22] When we talked, she cited a recent series on drug abuse in Bradenton as the kind of deep reporting that the paper likes to do to serve its community. The series was reproduced by other McClatchy-owned newspapers facing issues with drugs in their cities, indicating to Krauter the importance of the *Herald*'s stories.

The *Herald* reflects its owner's dedication to public service reporting. "High-quality journalism, of course, is the foundation of all that we do," wrote the McClatchy Company in its 2014 annual report. "Our news mission is part of McClatchy's proud, public-service legacy and it's also vital to our 21st century ambitions of retaining and growing our audiences."[23]

Krauter says that McClatchy does a lot to support the creation of meaningful accountability reporting at the *Herald* and its other properties. She says McClatchy has, for example, redesigned its newspapers' digital platform to make it easier to share multimedia content and provides ways for reporters at different papers to join forces on stories and share information. "We have weekly conference calls with all of the McClatchy newspapers where we share what we're working on," she says. "There's a good partnership there with the resources."[24] Krauter added that the McClatchy papers not only share information, but they often collaborate on national stories.

Thanks to that corporate support, as well as a commitment from local managers to public service reporting, the *Bradenton Herald* has turned out a steady stream of accountability journalism over the years studied. However, the percentage of front-page content consisting of public service journalism has fluctuated and seems to move up and down along with the state of the Florida economy. A summary of the paper's accountability reporting appears in Table 4-1, which shows a rise in the 1996 and 2001 samples, when the local economy was out of recession.

The amount of accountability reporting dropped in the later study years, from about 35 percent down to about 20 percent of front-page stories. It ended 2011 at the same percentage as it started in 1991. But in this paper's case, the raw numbers are important to examine as well. A detailed examination of the data shows that the *Herald* produced almost as many front-page accountability stories in 2011 as it did at its peak in 2001. The falling percentage is due to the fact that the *Herald* is putting more stories on its front pages (and generally not using wire copy on the front page, either). Although these figures imply that the *Herald* gave much of its front page to breaking news and original stories that had no link to government or policy, its editors clearly remain committed to the creation of original accountability stories despite limits in funding and staff size.

The *Herald* also does a respectable amount of digging for a paper of its size. Each year sampled had one deeply reported accountability story on the front page, except for 2011, which had two such stories. Most of these

TABLE 4-1. Total Accountability Reporting (classified as "Original Enterprise" and "Deep Accountability"), *Bradenton Herald*, Months of April, 1991–2011

Bradenton Herald	1991	1996	2001	2006	2011	Total
Total front-page stories	108	62	88	79	139	476
Total accountability stories	21	22	30	18	29	121
Simple/Deep	20 | 1	21 | 1	29 | 1	19 | 1	27 | 2	115 | 6
% Front-page accountability	20.37%	35.48%	34.09%	22.78%	20.86%	25.42%

stories dealt with local government actors, although one was written by the head of the *Herald*'s capital bureau and concerned a Florida state legislator from Bradenton.[25] The locally focused deep accountability reporting covered such topics as criminal justice[26] and government operations.[27] All the deeply reported accountability stories involved documents, some apparently leaked, some found through public record searches. None of the deep accountability stories dealt with nongovernmental actors, although one did ask why county officials gave work to rebuild bridges to a private contractor with a history of missing deadlines.[28]

I find the consistency of the *Herald*'s production of "deep watchdog" reporting to be most impressive. This kind of constant, sustained production of deep dive stories not only takes planning, but it also requires a long-term commitment by the editors to dedicating resources to this end. Krauter says that the data collected for this study only underlines that the *Herald*'s day-in, day-out attention to accountability reporting is bearing fruit, despite the staff cuts the paper has weathered. "It's amazing how much you can do with the resources dealt," she says.[29] She adds that one thing her paper has going for it is particular to Florida: The state has strong so-called "sunshine laws," which make it very simple for people to request government records and attend government meetings. "They get whittled at every year, but we are an open records state," she says. "The sunshine laws here are amazing."[30] She says it often takes just an oral request to get many records, although the paper tends to put its applications into writing.

Yet despite its commitment to accountability journalism, the *Herald* actually lost more than a third of its circulation between 2005 and 2013, before gaining back some ground with a 12 percent jump in 2014. McClatchy does not release financial information about its individual properties, so it is not possible to discuss in detail how that fall in circulation has affected the *Bradenton Herald*'s economic position. Krauter says the paper is currently profitable and has been profitable. The only financial figures publicly available come from the McClatchy Company's annual report for 2006, made just after the *Herald*'s acquisition, which state that the *Herald*'s revenues were $38 million in 2006 and nearly $36 million in 2005.[31] Although these figures are out of date, one would also have to believe that a chain like McClatchy would close any paper not turning a profit. For what it's worth, the high-tech website *Business Insider* named the *Bradenton Herald* to its 2011 list of "25 Newspapers That Have the Best Chance of Being Around in 10 Years."[32]

It is clear that because of the fall in circulation, *Herald* budgets were trimmed and staff was cut during the study period. Its high for the years studied was a newsgathering staff of ninety, according to Krauter. The whole McClatchy chain was hit hard by the world financial crisis and fired about one-third of its workforce in response.[33] The cuts at the *Bradenton Herald* seem even steeper than that, as Krauter says the news staff was down to between thirty and thirty-five people in 2015. And by mid-2017, the paper's staff directory showed just twenty-five people in the newsroom. But Krauter says the staff members she does have are young and energetic and often toil from early morning until late at night because they believe in what they do. "I love this newsroom," she says. "I've got a great team."[34] Many of the reporters spend a few years at the *Herald* gaining experience before moving on to larger papers, she adds, and their energy and enthusiasm push them to produce at high levels. As we will see next with the smallest of the papers, not every newsroom has the *Herald*'s ability to produce a steady stream of deep accountability reporting.

THE *LEWISTON TRIBUNE*—COMMUNITY CONNECTION

The *Lewiston Tribune*, founded in 1892, often mentions its watchdog role. "Newspapers are the only business mentioned in the Constitution," says Nathan Alford, editor and publisher of the paper, whose family has owned and edited the paper for five generations.[35] "The founding fathers saw the value of the Fourth Estate. We need good-quality, aggressive journalism today more than ever," he explains.[36] The paper's Facebook page seems to echo this idea; the wallpaper on its page for years shows the *Tribune*'s building, along with the quotation: "Inside these walls lies the most powerful freedom weapon in the world."[37] So as with other newspapers of small size, watchdog reporting remains at the heart of the *Tribune*'s mission.

Accordingly, the paper's top managers say they push reporters to dig into the work of government at all levels. "I think we do a good job particularly covering local government as well as county government, state government, *et cetera*, during the legislative session," says Doug Bauer, then the managing editor:

> A lot of what we're dealing with is government agencies sending out press releases and that being passed off as news. Well, for us, we want to find out what's beyond the press release, and that's where enterprise reporting and investigative reporting really separate us from the competition.[38]

He says that because the paper's readers are stretched over eight counties in two states and are both urban and rural dwellers, the *Tribune* takes a broad approach to its reporting overall. "We're kind of looking for stories that resonate throughout our readership area," he says. "When we report on something in a rural area, we want that to be a story that resonates for all of our readers—that it's something they can relate to."[39] Bauer says that the *Tribune* tries to put a solid enterprise story dealing with government accountability on its front pages once a week, as issues like crime, education, and environment are ones that have broad appeal for its readers. That may stand in contrast to the practice at a larger paper like the one in Atlanta, which shoots for an accountability story on the front page every day, but the *Journal-Constitution* has several times as many reporters on staff as the *Lewiston Tribune*.

The *Tribune* not only conceives of its watchdog role very much like that of the other newspapers studied here, but also its digital strategy is reminiscent of the larger newspapers examined. "The *Lewiston Tribune* prides itself on presenting old-school journalism in a new-school format, with a focus on local and regional stories," the newspaper writes on its Facebook page.[40] It was not only one of the first newspapers in the country to go online, but also Bauer says it was the second nationally to introduce a paywall. The *Lewiston Tribune* was getting about 1 million page views per month as of August 2015, he says, and the paper has thousands of followers on both Facebook and Twitter. Bauer says the paper's social media strategy is meant to drive people to the website and its other digital products, where their presence can be monetized. "My check is not signed by a guy named Zuckerberg," he jokes. "They're signed by our publisher, and that's where I want our readers to get their news—from our products."[41] The region's local flavor is also captured on the *Tribune*'s website with such features as a digital "brag board" where readers can submit pictures of their latest hunting or fishing success.

The *Lewiston Tribune* was chosen for this study for several reasons, including that when I started researching this book in 2011, it was one of the only very small newspapers in America to be available going back twenty years in digital form. At that time, many small newspapers had digital archives that went back only a handful of years rather than two full decades. In addition, the *Tribune* seemed representative of other small newspapers in terms of size and scope, and in its place as a vital resource for its readers. "What we do has so much value, day in and day out, in connecting people to their communities," says Alford.[42] The *Tribune* is the main source of local news in its area, though there are other news sources nearby. Lewiston has a television station—the CBS affiliate KLEW—and radio stations with news departments, but they do limited amounts of news. There is also another daily paper, the *Moscow-Pullman Daily News*, only twenty miles away, owned by the same small company that owns the *Lewiston Tribune*.

The area is remote and quiet compared with Bradenton. Lewiston is a scenic city in north central Idaho, approximately 200 miles south of the border with Canada. It is nestled on the border with Washington state, at the confluence of the Snake and Clearwater rivers—making it Idaho's only port. The area was first mapped by the explorers Meriwether Lewis and William Clark in 1805. Lewiston was formally founded in 1861, after gold was discovered nearby. The city had a 2016 population of approximately 32,840 residents, according to the Census Bureau.[43] Lewiston is the seat of Nez Perce County, population 40,000.[44] The county's demographics are somewhat similar to those of Manatee County, where Bradenton is located. Nez Perce County is 90 percent white, with a median 2015 household income of $48,000—except that the second-largest ethnic group in Lewiston is Native Americans, who make up nearly 6 percent of the county population. The area is home to the Nez Perce Indian Reservation, which stretches over five counties and has a population of approximately 18,000 people.[45] Lewiston is part of the Census Bureau's Lewiston–Clarkston "metropolitan statistical area," which stretches across the border into Washington and comprises more than 60,000 people.[46]

The *Lewiston Tribune* is by far the smallest of the nine newspapers studied, and its size seems to bring limitations on the amount of accountability reporting it does. Although the *Tribune* did just one piece of deep accountability reporting during the five months studied for this book, its editor makes it clear that watchdog journalism is done regularly. "We've been working on a series that's been going on for a few months now, kind of an occasional series, about mental health," says Bauer.[47] That said, only one of the 314 front-page *Tribune* stories analyzed for this book contained the kind of advanced reporting techniques that can be termed "deep" reporting as I have defined it—a 2011 story about the poor performance of Lewiston's newly appointed city manager in his previous job.[48] This suggests a strong correlation between budget size and the ability to put resources into deep reporting projects—which should worry anyone from a small city like Lewiston.

At first glance, it would seem easy to conclude that the *Tribune*'s staff was so small that it simply lacks the hands to undertake deep reporting consistently while also producing enough copy to fill the newspaper and the website every day. Its total staff as of August 2015 was about thirty-five people, according to Bauer, including editors, reporters, and news assistants. About twelve of those people were reporters, he says. That's about one-third the size of the staff at the *Bradenton Herald*, although the *Tribune* added more staff later on. By mid-2017, the *Tribune* had more than sixty people in its staff directory, including more than thirty in newsgathering.

As at the larger papers, *Tribune* editors try to free up reporters to pursue deep reporting projects, but Bauer admits that releasing reporters from their beats is difficult to do. "With a small staff, that doesn't mean that they just get to write the next two weeks off their calendar and just go down the rabbit hole," he explains. "They still need to cover their bases to a certain degree, but we try to do as much as we can to give them the flexibility to do those big issue stories because it's important."[49] The fact that the *Tribune* had very little deep reporting whatsoever in the study sample while the larger papers all had a steady diet of "deep watchdog" stories suggests that the smallest American newspapers face considerable obstacles in creating accountability reporting, particularly the kind of deep reporting that is the focus of this study.

Still, the *Lewiston Tribune* managed to turn out a fair amount of "simple enterprise" reporting that shed light on policy issues and the work of government. Interestingly, the paper not only covered the work of local governments in both Idaho and Washington, but also of the three smallest papers studied, it had the highest number of stories that focused on federal government agencies (twenty stories at the *Tribune* as opposed to sixteen at the *Albany Times Union* and twelve at the *Bradenton Herald*). Over the study period, the *Lewiston Tribune* gave a significant amount of attention to the federal Interior Department, which runs the Nez Perce National Forest and the Nez Perce Historical Park, both outside Lewiston. The paper also gave extensive coverage to the federal departments of Agriculture and Defense, as the Army Corps of Engineers has been running numerous projects in the rivers near Lewiston. It is important that local newspapers continue to do this kind of coverage of the federal government, which adds something over what newspapers can accomplish in Washington, D.C. As Table 4–2 demonstrates, the total amount of "simple enterprise" stories at the *Tribune* over the study period averaged 25 percent of front-page stories, with a high of 40 percent in 2001 and a low of 15 percent in 1996. The total amount of "simple enterprise" stories in the *Tribune* sample was just about the same as at the *Bradenton Herald* (where "simple enterprise" was 24 percent of front-page stories).

TABLE 4-2. "Simple Enterprise" Stories, *Lewiston Tribune*, Months of April, 1991–2011

Lewiston Tribune	1991	1996	2001	2006	2011	Total
Total number of "simple enterprise" stories	16	9	22	17	17	81
Total front-page stories	72	59	54	60	69	314
% of Total front-page stories that are "simple enterprise"	22.22%	15.25%	40.74%	28.33%	24.64%	25.80%

Still, there were great variations in the amount of "simple enterprise" reporting being done at the *Lewiston Tribune* in different years. The rise in "simple enterprise" stories to about 40 percent of front-page stories in 2001, as the Internet came to be widely used, suggests that the technology could have been useful in encouraging original non-news reporting. And the subsequent drop in the percentage of "simple enterprise" stories in the later samples to 28 percent in 2006 and 24 percent in 2011 suggests that smaller staffs and tighter budgets did limit the amount of original enterprise reporting being done.

The drop in original enterprise reporting over time also suggests that small papers like the *Tribune* must focus on news if there are few other sources for breaking news in their communities. "It's a *news* paper and giving them news is what our model is all about," Bauer stresses. But, that said, he echoes the words of another small-paper editor, Joan Krauter of the *Bradenton Herald*, in praising the work of his staff. "Pound for pound, we produce as much content as any paper I've ever seen," he says.[50] He also commends the paper's owners, for whom the paper is not just a business, but also a labor of love. "We're very passionate about what we do, and feel very strongly about our role," Bauer says. "I think there's still a bright future ahead for us as long as we maintain and build upon standards that have been laid out before by those who came before us."[51] Although the data suggests that the need to produce news and to fill the *Lewiston Tribune* print and online editions with copy does not leave much time for deep dive reporting, there can be no question that its owners and staff are deeply committed to running a news organization that approaches its work with seriousness, ambition, and community spirit.

CONCLUSIONS ABOUT THE SMALL NEWSPAPER GROUP

The U.S. government's concern about the role of information in local communities, which was voiced in the landmark FCC report, can be both assuaged and heightened by the data gathered for this part of the nine-newspaper study. Although one of the small papers examined produced a steady flow of watchdog journalism, the near-absence of deep reporting at the other during the five months studied in depth is a cause for concern. There are several thousand daily and weekly newspapers in America that are similar in circulation to or even smaller than the *Lewiston Tribune*, and they would seem to face serious obstacles to the production of public service journalism, particularly deep accountability reporting, because of their small size and limited resources. Common sense suggests, and the data backs up the notion, that small newspapers like the ones analyzed here are the most vulnerable to the vagaries of the economy.

But if there is any good news here, it is that one of the two papers profiled in this chapter might be said to produce more accountability reporting than expected. The *Bradenton Herald* has managed to create a steady stream of "deep watchdog" stories over time, despite its small staff. The paper's editor says it does so by pushing its reporters to "act bigger" than the paper really is. She says that the ways the *Herald* does this include placing the production of accountability journalism in reporters' annual goals and by creating ways to free reporters from daily reporting to pursue those deep reporting projects. This suggests that paper leadership *can* make a difference when it comes to the creation of watchdog reporting. When management makes original enterprise reporting and deep accountability reporting a priority and dedicates resources to it, these crucial watchdog and original enterprise stories get written.

The data also suggests that corporate ownership can be helpful for smaller papers. At the *Herald*, owner McClatchy has encouraged the creation of accountability reporting by dedicating extra resources to it and by creating information-sharing systems that assist their properties in working together. The fact that the *Lewiston Tribune* had little deep accountability reporting during the months studied does not mean that independent papers do not create such reporting, for they clearly do. But it suggests that small papers that are part of large ownership groups reap benefits from the additional resources that their corporate parents are able to provide, even when the benefits are not monetary—such as being able to trade story ideas with other newspapers. Overall, the data for this cohort suggests that any paper in America, no matter how small, can create some deep accountability reporting, even if it has a tiny staff and limited financial resources—and that even the smallest papers believe that watchdog reporting is a key part of their mission. And this is very good news, indeed.

CHAPTER 5

If Not Now, When?

This work has aspired to uncover essential truths about the news business today through data and analysis. I have tried to present empirical evidence gathered in a credible and replicable way to answer key questions about the way in which newspapers cover government, policy issues, civil society, and business. My hope is that this analysis, because it is so broad and stretches over such a long time period, makes some valuable points about the content of newspapers as they adapted to digital technologies. So while this is an academic work, I implore members of the press to think about these results and to apply their lessons to their journalism. I also hope consumers of news will also gain newfound respect for the importance of real, deep, meaningful accountability journalism from the points raised in this discussion.

There is an even more personal reason why I undertook this project: my years in Russia. I have been studying Russia for a quarter-century and lived there, working as a journalist, from 1992 to 2006. During that time, I saw the Russian media follow an arc from state control to freedom and, sadly, mostly back to state control. In late Soviet days, journalists could criticize low-ranking members of the government, but not the leadership. After the Soviet Union fell apart in 1991, Russian President Boris Yeltsin generally left the press unfettered by government interference during his years in power. Under his rule, the Russian journalists enjoyed the freedom to monitor government in a way they had never had before. Russian society was far better for it, as the press turned its spotlight on corruption, bad policies, and incompetence.

But since Vladimir Putin came into power on the last day of 1999, the watchdog role has been all but eviscerated. While there are still independent newspapers and websites today, the single largest source of information for Russian citizens—television—is controlled by the state, either through direct ownership, quasi-governmental ownership, or Kremlin-friendly owners. Most Russian journalists today have to toe the government's line in order to keep their jobs, and many now self-censor to avoid trouble with the authorities. Other than on the Internet, there is little watchdog reporting. Those who do try to report on government wrongdoing risk their lives in doing so.

The larger effect of Russian government control over the media and frequent violence against journalists has been to crush the tradition of independent monitoring of the government by the press. As one American reporter teaching journalism classes in the Russian city of Rostov-on-Don found out firsthand, young Russian journalists coming up in the Putin era simply lack an accountability mindset:

> One of the first things I asked the students was to name the biggest problem in Rostov. They burst out, almost in unison: "Corruption"—both political and economic. "So what are you all doing about it?" I wanted to know. They responded with blank stares. They pointed out that their local media doesn't even publish or air major *features* of individual businesses, let alone probes. Replicate that situation hundreds of times, all across Russia, and you've got the big picture.[1]

Despite the work of many courageous reporters and bloggers in Russia, the lack of a truly free and vibrant press as part of a system of checks and balances is having major repercussions in Russian society. The lack of a watchdog press is one of the factors that have led to the rise of authoritarianism again. The press can guard against abuse of power only if it is independent of that power, which is not the case in Russia.

However, in the United States our media are free of direct government control, and despite all the financial issues, the vast majority of news organizations are still financially sound. Because of my experience in Russia, I have little sympathy for an American press that fails to make the most of its watchdog role. I have seen the results on society of the lack of accountability reporting, and it is not pretty. Our watchdogs—particularly our newspapers—are one of America's most valuable assets. "It would be interesting to see if every newspaper in the country just didn't publish for a single day," muses Doug Bauer of the *Lewiston Tribune*. "I think people would recognize where their news actually comes from. Because I don't think people collectively in this country recognize or realize how much reporting happens at newspapers, and how that feeds other media outlets."[2] Happily, this study suggests that American newspapers still take their watchdog role very seriously, despite many challenges.

ALL IS NOT LOST

Back in 2009, when the worst effects of the financial crisis were hitting American newspapers, Princeton professor Paul Starr worried in the pages of *The New Republic* about whether economically weakened papers would still be able to carry out their watchdog role:

> More than any other medium, newspapers have been our eyes on the state, our check on private abuses, our civic alarm systems. It is true that they have often failed to perform those functions as well as they should have. But whether they can continue to perform them at all is now in doubt.[3]

One of the key findings of this work is that despite their economic problems, American newspapers *do* continue to be a watchdog over the government and, to a lesser extent, business. The aggregated results from across the nine-newspaper study show that the amount of deep accountability reporting overall across the newspapers studied has generally increased, not decreased, over the two decades studied. This would seem to refute the fear expressed by numerous editors and scholars that newspapers have been so adversely affected by financial issues that they are unable to perform the watchdog role. I know that many newspaper editors and reporters who will read this book have seen cutbacks at their papers and feel as if they are doing less digging than they used to do. The data certainly does contain some rather troubling findings, including that accountability coverage at the papers moved to a more narrow range of topics over time, with more reliance on government sources and less willingness to take on issues involving systemic wrongdoing. Still, the worries of experts like Professor Starr seem not to have materialized across the board.

The data from this representative selection of newspapers suggests that though the total amount of public service journalism has dropped at some news outlets, others have redeployed resources to accountability reporting and increased the amounts that they produce. Not only did the total number of accountability stories increase overall between 1991 and 2011, but the total amount of *deep* accountability articles increased during this period as well. This refutes the conventional wisdom and previous research, which suggests that watchdog reporting is dying out in this era of small staffs, tight money, and short attention spans.

Moreover, the large jump in "deep watchdog" stories in several of the papers studied—those in Washington, D.C., Atlanta, Denver, and Minneapolis—suggests that it is metropolitan dailies that are most likely to continue to be the engines driving accountability reporting forward. These are the papers operating in a competitive local media environment, and so they have been pressed to deliver more than their competitors in order to draw readers. They also have more resources available than nearly every local news nonprofit. Luckily for their communities, these metropolitan papers are choosing to use their considerable resources to create accountability reporting, often producing the kinds of deeply reported stories their smaller rivals lack the resources to produce. This has been driven by a desire to survive, not by altruism, but it is one of the few positive consequences of a financial crisis that has hit newspapers hard.

That some newspapers are actually better watchdogs than they used to be tells us that editors can turn news organizations into large producers of accountability reporting by making oversight of the government a priority. The *Atlanta Journal-Constitution* is the poster child for the transformation of newspapers into lean, mean reporting machines in this way. Its front-page output in 1991 was mostly breaking news and wire stories. But its front pages in 2011 were chock-full of accountability stories. This paper changed its content greatly as a result of the will of its editors and an emphasis on listening to readers. I can find nothing that makes the *Journal-Constitution* unique as a newsgathering organization, nor about Atlanta as a subject. The *AJC* simply applied elbow grease in the right places because it believed its readers when surveys said they wanted more accountability reporting. The growth in the paper's circulation in response is heartening. It suggests that readers are indeed attracted by serious reporting about their most important institutions.

Yet at the same time, many newspapers' ability to produce deep and meaningful accountability journalism has fallen in recent years, likely because they have been limited by a lack of staff and other resources. To understand this point, consider that only four of the nine newspapers studied had their highest percentage of "deep watchdog" reporting in the 2011 sample. That means that something drove down the percentage of "deep watchdog" reports at several of the papers after it had been higher. The drop-off at the large papers does not worry me too much, because these nationally focused papers still do significant amounts of accountability reporting. But any reduction of deep accountability reporting at the small newspapers is more concerning because they start at such a low baseline and remain essential to the proper functioning of democracy at a local level.

The data presented here confirms the concerns of the FCC that watch-dog reporting remains "at risk" at many local newspapers.[4] The three smallest newspapers studied for this book—the Albany, Bradenton, and Lewiston papers—lacked any deep investigations of nongovernmental actors in their samples, including businesses, NGOs, and other public policy players outside of government. The data also suggests a strong correlation between resource levels and accountability output, suggesting it is difficult for small papers to muster the resources for much deep account-ability reporting. This is an important finding, as America has hundreds of small newspapers that must do watchdog reporting to serve their com-munities but undoubtedly have scant resources to dedicate to it. This is a problem that is not likely to go away any time soon, as the pressure increases on small papers to do more digitally with the same amount of resources they had for print, or less.

A HUGE JOB TO DO

Despite the fact that all the papers studied and, in reality, virtually all the news organizations in America cover the work of government to a high degree, vast parts of the bureaucracy are going unstudied or understudied. Even if every news organization in America were to make a concerted effort to cover the bureaucracy, very little work of government would actu-ally receive meaningful coverage because there are thousands of entities. The problem is even more acute because many local newspapers have few resources available for the production of accountability reporting. To me, the fact that the judiciary garnered very little coverage at any level by the news organizations studied—less than 3 percent of total accountability stories studied—is particularly worrisome, as is the relatively light cover-age of intelligence issues (which were less than 1 percent of the total). That two key parts of our government garner little attention from the media shows how difficult it is for the news industry to serve as an effective watch-dog over all essential governmental functions.

Not only are there a lot of such functions to cover, but also government operations are often complex and require a build-up of expertise and con-tacts over time. For instance, take a simple function like banking. There are actually three U.S. government agencies that regulate banks (the Fed-eral Reserve Bank, the Office of the Comptroller of the Currency, and the Federal Deposit Insurance Corporation), and another eight agencies involved in financial regulation more generally.[5] Graphics that illustrate how financial regulation works look like a large and tangled web. As Dean Starkman points out in his excellent analysis of why the media missed the world financial crisis, it takes time and effort for a reporter to learn how financial regulation really works in the United States, given the number of players and the complexity of the process.[6] And most papers have only the ability to send reporters to bore down into the most relevant public policy questions at any one time.

Moreover, systemic issues involving government are often incredibly hard stories to report. It is much more straightforward to critique how a specific agency deals with a specific public policy problem than to deal with a wholesale failure. It takes an experienced journalist, given lots of time to work, to nail these kinds of articles. Often, the reporter needs to combine many sources to get the story right. My own experience is that this kind of work often develops like a mosaic, coming into focus only after many individual pieces of information are put together systematically. Such stories are not only hard to conceptualize and difficult to report, but they sometimes run into issues because they bump up against politics. Many a journalist has been accused of playing politics by the subject of an accountability article after critical coverage, even if the reporter has made every effort to stay objective. Again, judging from my own experience, the digital revolution has made news organizations particularly aware of demonstrating biases in their reporting, because they know it is now easier than ever for angry article subjects and readers to kick up a fuss when they believe reporting is unfair. The tradition of U.S. newspapers to stick to objective journalism is another important reason why their accountability reporting is so important to our political process and resonates with so many readers.

Many critics have suggested that the U.S. media have been "asleep at the wheel" as of late and have failed to cover numerous public policy issues properly like the causes of the 2007 financial crisis, but this criticism oversimplifies the task at hand. The size of the government in the United States has grown to such a degree that one would need an army of journalists just to monitor its work. There were about 22 million people working in federal, state, and local government as of 2016—about two-thirds of whom work on the local level.[7] This is more than 5 percent of the U.S. population. So tens of thousands of journalists are necessary to keep an eye on all those people. It would be an enormous task, even for a hungry and active watchdog media.

Also worrisome is the relatively low level of investigation of business revealed by this study. Nearly every news organization studied had few accountability stories focusing on nongovernmental actors, suggesting that there are too few eyes on the business community and NGOs involved in policy issues. Furthermore, the number of business sources being quoted in accountability articles fell significantly in the later study years, reflecting falling interest or ability to hold the business sector accountable.[8] Arguably, of the news organizations studied, only the *Wall Street Journal* focuses on business and industry. This is inadequate given the huge role that business and money play in U.S. society today—particularly under a Trump presidency.

The huge size of the bureaucracy and the military-industrial complex, and the sheer complexity of the task of assessing large-scale public policies, means that editors have to be strategic about what to bring under scrutiny, and they need to build the expertise necessary to complete that scrutiny in a way that matters. With so many different layers of government, it is impossible to act as an effective watchdog over them all. So how do newspapers choose where to focus? Sometimes breaking news dictates what news organizations will cover. Other times, reporters are offered leaked documents or other information that leads to a report. But there rarely seems to be strategy involved. The news nonprofit ProPublica offers an interesting model for covering business–government relations, because it has chosen a few key issues as its main focus. Setting clear priorities or choosing particular topics for concentration would probably improve accountability reporting at most news organizations. The choice would depend on the paper and on which actors and issues are most relevant.

In addition to being more strategic about what to cover, editors have to be more thoughtful about how they deploy their resources into accountability reporting. If there is one thing that is clearly demonstrated by this research, it is that individual editors can have a huge impact on what their papers cover and how they cover it. The papers at which editors made a clearly stated commitment to accountability reporting and tried to create systems to drive coverage were able to produce deep investigative and watchdog reports at high levels despite their having limited staff and money to do so. I hope this study will remind editors of their key role in this crucial process.

I have already spoken about this paper, but the *Atlanta Journal-Constitution* really shows how it should be done. In 1991, it did not do a lot of enterprise reporting, and it certainly did not dig deep. But by 2011, that had all changed. The *AJC*, assuming the April 2011 sample was no fluke—and I have every reason to believe it is an accurate representation of the paper's changing priorities, given my discussion with editor Kevin Riley—had morphed into a vibrant watchdog, with nine "deep watchdog" reports in just one month. That represents a huge investment of reporter time. In response, the paper's circulation has increased in recent years as it has upgraded its content. This suggests a path forward for the newspaper industry and, to a lesser extent, for online news organizations. Quality still sells. The *Minneapolis Star Tribune* and *The Denver Post* also deserve shout-outs for managing to keep their focus on meaningful, deep accountability reporting during the study period despite the financial challenges. These papers, too, provide an example about how to serve one's community through accountability reporting.

I also find myself impressed by the *Albany Times Union*. Yes, as the largest paper in New York's capital region, the paper has a built-in focus and audience. But the *Atlanta Journal-Constitution*, *The Denver Post*, and, for all intents and purposes, the *Minneapolis Star Tribune* are also located in their state capitals (the Minnesota state capital is St. Paul, adjacent to Minneapolis). Yet the *ATU*, a much smaller paper, beat those larger newspapers on numerous metrics, like in the percentage of front-page deep accountability stories. The *Times Union* is a terrific paper, and one that can rival news organizations several times its size, even if it is not digging quite as much as it used to do. The study results certainly suggest that even small newspapers can do excellent watchdog reporting if they make doing so a priority. The challenge is to keep watchdog reporting flowing as resources continue to shrink and competition from online organizations increases. Some of the papers studied, like *The Denver Post*, have definitely struggled to keep quality high in the years since my data collection finished, as staff size has continued to dwindle.

MANY CHALLENGES AHEAD

Despite the critical importance of watchdog reporting, its road going forward looks fairly rocky. Some of the issues identified here are systemic in nature and have been around since the start of the digital revolution. One of these is the need for "clicks." We all know the sites that try to generate reader interest with articles that spread like wildfire on Facebook—stories like "18 Things Every Guy with Sisters Has Experienced" and "You Have to Hear What Kanye Told Kim About Their Kids." The fact of the matter is that light fare often generates more clickthroughs than serious journalism. The editors I interviewed said uniformly that most accountability reporting garners far fewer clicks than more entertaining fare. The election of 2016 added a new corollary—that "fake news" can perform better online than real news.[9] News organizations have to remain committed to accountability journalism, even if it is not likely to play well digitally, because it's really the thing that matters the most in journalism. It would be better to experiment with new ways to engage readers rather than to back away from public service journalism.

Another similar systemic and related issue facing news organizations today is that too many journalists spend their time parroting one another's coverage, repeating facts that others have already reported instead of spending their time to break their own stories. This is another result of the need for clicks. "Every news organization thinks it needs its own take on any story so it can fill its own page and have a place for its own ad and get its own page view and earn its own pennies for each one," explains one of the most astute observers of journalism in the Internet Age, Professor Jeff Jarvis of the City University of New York's Graduate School of Journalism.[10] And it is essential to public policy that this attitude be changed and news organizations refocus on original enterprise journalism.

I am far from alone in pointing out these systemic problems. The former head of my old research center at Harvard, the esteemed Pulitzer Prize–winning journalist Alex Jones, has stressed the importance of the "iron core" of journalism.[11] Jarvis explains the same need in more economic terms:

> We do need to shift news from a news business based on volume to one based on value: unique value to the people and communities it serves. The salvation of this profession that I hold dear and necessary can come only from a flight to quality: doing the reporting that no one else is doing; serving people's needs with substance rather than momentary distraction; helping to improve our lives and communities; surprising, engaging, enlightening, and educating the public. We will measure our worth not with old, mass-media metrics that count page views, unique users, and eyeballs by the ton. It will come with measurements of impact and value.[12]

Impact and value are what accountability journalism is all about. In the long run, it's also good business.

Some of the other problems faced today by watchdog journalism are being badly exacerbated by the Trump presidency. It is a huge challenge that America has elected a chief executive who expresses his hatred for the news media on a regular basis, particularly organizations doing accountability reporting that is in any way critical of him. "Trump has consistently trampled on America's First Amendment tradition," wrote Joel Simon, head of the Committee to Protect Journalists, which took the unprecedented step of labeling Trump an official threat to press freedom. "Trump has insulted and vilified the press and called individual journalists dishonest and sleazy," Simon continued. "He has systematically denied press credentials to outlets who have covered him critically. . . . [H]e clearly intends to make trouble for the media and would doubtless find a way to do so."[13] A president who has little respect for a watchdog press, even though he owes much of his success to media coverage, is an affront to the Founding Fathers who created freedom of the press as a counterweight to government power over 200 years ago. Trump and many of his colleagues would be happy to see accountability journalism fade away entirely. That is why it is so critical to our society today that the watchdog press perform exactly that role, and perform it with newfound zeal. The administration's current hostility to critical journalism shows precisely why the American press was imbued with freedom, and why the American legal system has upheld the press's wide right to criticize public figures. No blogger or auto-mated newswriting program has the power of a major American news-paper to keep our elected and unelected officials in the spotlight.

Another issue exacerbated by Trump's presidential run is citizens' loss of confidence in the news media. The Gallup organization recently reported that trust in the media is at its lowest point since it started polling on this topic in 1972.[14] In a December 2016 Gallup survey, only 32 percent of respondents and 14 percent of the Republicans indicated "a great deal" or "a fair amount" of trust in the media.[15] The fact that so many Republicans now distrust the "lamestream" media is surely one of the reasons why Trump won the election. This distrust allowed many Trump supporters to ignore or discount alarming reports indicating he had sexually harassed women and acted unethically in his business dealings. It is important to note that Gallup found that mistrust of the media by Republicans was about 32 percent in late 2015, meaning it dropped by more than half during the year that Trump was running for president.[16] By bashing the press, the Republican establishment is clearly trying to circumvent the critical eye of reporters so it can better use its own information channels to reach citi-zens. This has worked well for Republican candidates, but badly for American democracy, which has become increasingly polarized over the past twenty-five years.[17] Good public policy requires politicians to work across the aisle, but this has become less likely as the political parties have moved further away from each other in their central beliefs.

Because many people no longer trust reporters, and because information now flows so freely around them, we have moved into what critics have termed a "post-factual society."[18] This emphasis on what the comedian Stephen Colbert calls "truthiness" rather than truth itself poses consider-able challenges for watchdog journalism. A media ecosystem where facts do not matter, or can be easily ignored, or easily neutralized by lies, threat-ens our entire society by undermining the basis for making good public policy decisions. This situation has been made worse by the advent of the

Internet, where anything can be published, whether it is true or not. And social media have added to the problem by spreading "false news" easily, and by being a place where automated "bots" can spew out propaganda in high quantities. If that weren't enough, cable news stations like Fox News Channel also pour gasoline on the proverbial fire by focusing on opinion rather than fact. These massive changes in how information is presented and filtered have set the entire world of journalism on its head. This has led to panicked head scratching by many media analysts, including this one, about the role of media today.

Rather than try to figure out how to save journalism—which is far beyond what I can do here, as the subject will fill many books yet to come—I would like to focus on what the latest changes in the media landscape mean for watchdog journalism. Although the situation I have outlined here would seem to bode very badly for accountability journalism, I would argue that there is actually great opportunity now for America's news media, particularly its newspapers, to reassert their role as the engine that drives public policy debate through fact-based reporting. The more angry people get about officials' trying to get away with lies, the more likely they are to turn to factual, verified reporting. Millions may have tuned out, but millions more people are now tuning in, as evidenced by the "Trump bump" raising news consumption and subscription numbers in recent months.[19] The Trump presidency provides everything that journalists need to reinforce their role as the "iron core" of American society, and I remain convinced, as do many others, that it is the verification function of journalism that ensures it will continue to play a key role in a world where information is plentiful, but not always credible. That is why it is critically important that editors strengthen public affairs journalism in the coming years, and why news consumers support their efforts with their dollars and their eyeballs. The only way watchdog journalism will survive and protect the citizenry is if it is both produced and consumed. To quote one of the great Jewish sages, Hillel, "And if not now, when?"[20]

RECOMMENDATIONS

I know this will not be easy. But I hope most of all that this book will remind reporters and editors of the importance of the watchdog role, and that it will inspire them to redouble their efforts to use the power of the press where it is needed most. Every editor interviewed for this book enunciated in strong and forceful terms the need for his or her newspaper to be a watchdog over the government. I hope that this work also reminds consumers that they hold the key to the production of meaningful public service journalism. The more of it that is consumed, the more it will continue to be produced.

To that end, I present ten recommendations resulting from this research. I make them to newspaper editors, as they are most likely to drive the changes needed to make public service journalism all that it can be. I feel certain that any news organization implementing these recommendations will produce more accountability reporting and more deep investigative and watchdog reporting, than ever before. This is the most important work a news organization can do. And it is also good business. To readers, I add just one more recommendation: Subscribe to your local paper. Even better: subscribe to both a local and a nationally focused newspaper. Spending money to support the work of newspapers is one of the best investments you will ever make in your quality of life and the quality of our democracy.

1. **Make deep accountability reporting for your particular audience a priority.** The reason we have a free press is not really to share celebrity gossip, "fabricated" news items, or cute cat videos. Its first and foremost responsibility is to safeguard the people from abuses of power. The experience of numerous news organizations covered by this research suggests that increasing accountability reporting can actually spur readership and drive customers to pay for their papers' work. To do so, news organizations must focus on the needs of their particular community. "What do they need from you? What do they expect from you?" asks Marcus Brauchli of the *Washington Post* and the *Wall Street Journal*. "Figure out whom you're serving and what you're serving them. And be really true to that. If you don't know who you are, they won't know who you are."[21] New analytic tools make it easier than ever to interact with the audience to figure out exactly which accountability issues are of the most importance, and new digital tools provide myriad ways to tell those stories in compelling ways.

2. **Make sure readers know that accountability reporting is your priority.** News organizations need to state that accountability journalism is a top priority. Such statements should be prominent in both print and digital versions of the paper and in social media, to remind readers just how important this work is to the citizenry. This seems elementary, but few of the papers studied actually have a mission statement or a written policy on the importance of watchdog journalism where it can be easily seen by its audience. It should also be front and center in marketing materials, as it can serve as a potent selling point for potential subscribers and advertisers.

3. **Examine the production system for accountability reporting and whatever it is, improve it.** The newspapers studied here have generally developed systems that encourage their reporters to come up with ideas for

deep accountability articles and to free them up to produce such stories. It is important for news organizations to encourage all reporters, not just those on investigative beats, to come up with ideas for deep accountability reports and to complete them. Many of the papers studied have created ways for reporters to step off their beat for a few days or even a few weeks to pursue deep reporting projects. Some also put deep reporting projects into reporters' written goals for the year. Editors have to allow reporters to invest time in reporting that might not turn into an article at all, or into an article soon. Training all staff in how to do Freedom of Information Act requests and the basics of data journalism were suggested by several of the editors interviewed.

4. **Focus on multiple levels and branches of government.** News organizations need to make sure that they are examining the work of all three branches of the U.S. government as well as some of the autonomous agencies that have daily impact on the quality of their readers' lives. Even a local paper can report accountability stories that involve the federal government and state government, both of which touch the lives of their readers. This analysis has found scant coverage of some of the most important parts of American government—in particular the judicial branch, which received little attention by any news organization in the study period. If every American newspaper made sure to address government accountability on federal, state, and local levels, our national accountability portrait would be far more complete. The reach of the federal government is too large for its oversight to be left to a few national news organizations.

5. **Remember that accountability journalism needs to focus on business as well as government, as the two are so intertwined.** This study found relatively low levels of inquiry targeting the role of companies and corporations in the policymaking process. This is most unfortunate, given the interplay between business and government. As Woodward and Bernstein did when they were reporting on Watergate, reporters today would be well served to "follow the money." This could not be more true now that a businessman with interests all over the world is in the White House—particularly given his penchant for hiring cabinet members with close ties to business.

6. **Seek expertise.** Independent experts are not only good to quote in stories to add context, but often they have deep knowledge of their subject areas. In order to sniff out stories, reporters not only need a network of contacts, but also they need to get into the habit of interviewing people just to flesh out story ideas. I worry about reporters' moving away from telephone and face-to-face contact, given how I see student journalists work today. My students prefer doing interviews by e-mail or text, and

they sometimes push back when I explain that there is no substitute for a personal meeting.

Journalists also need to refocus their reporting efforts on finding independent experts to quote in stories, to help evaluate the information being presented. Reliance on government sources has increased over the years for many reasons, one being that government sources are often easy to reach, and their social media presences often make them more quotable than before. But it is the verification function of the media that is often most useful, and that means going to sources outside the government frequently and exercising healthy skepticism about government statements.

7. **Engage readers more when looking for accountability ideas.** This is one of the few areas where I think television stations might have an advantage over newspapers, as many of them have "tip lines" and actively solicit viewers to submit story ideas. Although it is perfectly easy to contact a newspaper, not all papers make it clear to readers that their input on stories, particularly in the area of investigations and watchdog reporting, is welcome. A link on the home page specifically seeking accountability ideas and more frequent outreach about watchdog reporting on social media might spur more valuable input from readers, as well as from current and former government workers with whistles to blow.

8. **Use data journalism and the possibilities of the Internet to bolster accountability reporting.** Newspapers need to continue to embrace the many possibilities put forward by the Internet in general and data journalism in particular—not only to inform readers, but also as a strategic tool in creating meaningful accountability journalism. Yes, it is challenging to find people with the computer, visual arts, and journalism skills to create good data journalism. But the presence of so many jobs in this area is spurring new data journalism–training programs at universities around the United States. Of course, it is generally the larger papers that will be able to hire these specialists, but they are within reach of small papers as well. Even for those without dedicated specialists, there are more and more tools available online, free of charge, to create timelines, interactive graphics, and other useful data-based projects. These tools can be even more powerful than text for some stories.

9. **Partner up, particularly with nonprofit journalism organizations.** News nonprofits are doing some terrific journalism. Newspapers need to understand that these online news organizations can often become viable partners. A newspaper might not want to partner with a direct competitor doing general news, but many online news organizations have a different mission from their city's newspapers and therefore could offer expertise or a new perspective. There are synergies here to explore. Some of the most

compelling journalism of recent years, like the prize-winning 2016 "Panama Papers" project, resulted from collaborative journalism.

10. **Instill in reporters a mindset that they need to be skeptical without being cynical.** This is perhaps the single most challenging recommendation, but ultimately the most important. Reporters of my generation already know the importance of accountability reporting. But I worry about the young reporters coming up, as I teach at a university and see how the mindset of young people today differs from my own. This is not to say that we're all good and they're all bad. Far from it. But the generations of people who know only the digital world have grown up with different perceptions of what is important than those of us who predate the Internet revolution. My own students don't generally consume newspapers or watch documentaries, even though many of them plan careers in journalism. They would rather click on links on Facebook promising a quick laugh, than a serious groan. This means that journalism programs at the high school, college, and graduate levels have to make sure that all students understand that their number one responsibility is to shed light on abuses of power. That may be a hard sell to the young woman who wants to work in the beauty department of a magazine or the young man who wants to be a sports blogger. But I cannot think of a better way to make sure that the next generation of journalists is prepared to take on their most important task. The state of our republic ultimately depends on it. As the *Guardian* so eloquently put it, "Without journalism, there is no America."[22]

EPILOGUE

The data collection for this book stretches only to 2011. In the best of all possible worlds, I would have had the time before publication to extend my data collection to the next five-year data point, 2016. Having one more data set would have helped me assess how additional aspects of the digital revolution have affected the production of accountability journalism, particularly the rise of social media, and to have assessed fully the effects of the unprecedented election of 2016. While I almost certainly will do such research as a follow-up project, to do so for this book was not possible because of its tight publication schedule. That said, allow me to posit what those 2016 results might show—and why an examination of 2017 and beyond would likely turn out very different from what I found for the early Internet era.

My best guess is that if this analysis were to be replicated for April 2016, the quantities of deep watchdog reporting would approximate those for 2011. After all, by 2011, the nine newspapers studied already seemed dedicated to producing about as much accountability reporting as they could muster. I see little reason to think that any of the editors lost their taste for accountability reporting during the next five years. In fact, the appetite might have been greater in 2016 than it was five years earlier, because it was an election year and also the last chance to dig into the work of the Obama administration. Yet at the same time, a few of the papers were leaner in 2016 than they had been in 2011, which might have lessened the papers' ability to produce deep dive reporting, even though editors remained dedicated to it. Some of the papers studied here, particularly *The Denver Post*, went through some additional staff cuts after 2011, which might have driven down the amount and quality of the accountability reporting being done despite management's commitment to it.[23]

The one clear exception to this line of thinking is the *Washington Post*, which likely had even more accountability reporting in 2016 than in 2011 because of a significant increase in its reporting staff. As I discussed in Chapter 2, billionaire owner Jeff Bezos started investing considerable funds soon after he purchased the *Post* in 2013, allowing the paper to add dozens of reporting positions. This would seem a likely reason to suspect the *Post* contains more accountability journalism in 2016 than five years earlier, particularly given the importance in Washington of the presidential election. The quality and breadth of the reporting in the *Post* overall seems to this casual reader of the newspaper to have improved noticeably over the past few years, thanks at least in part to Bezos's infusion of funds.

Just before I sent this book to press, I had the good fortune to chat with *Washington Post* editor Marty Baron at an awards dinner we were both attending.[24] Bezos's investment in the *Post*, Baron said, had significantly strengthened the paper's ability to do deep watchdog stories. Nevertheless, he said, the *Post* was still trying to innovate to find still better ways to create this most important kind of journalism. For instance, Baron said, he was in the process of putting together a new quick-strike investigative reporting team. While the current group of regular investigative reporters would continue to do the kind of watchdog stories that took many months to complete, Baron said this new team would immerse itself in just one story at a time. Its goal is to turn out a deep investigation of a hot topic in just a week or two. And Baron said that more than 500 people had applied for the eight spots on this new team.

That said, were my research to be repeated in 2017 or 2021, I would have every reason to believe that the quantities of accountability reporting would increase over 2011, not only at the *Washington Post*, but also at most, if not all, of the nine newspapers studied. Part of this would be in response to what *Mother Jones* has called "the most bizarre election we've ever seen."[25] Donald Trump's presidency, simply put, is a game changer when it comes to watchdog reporting. "Independent accountability journalism is gaining new support among many Americans mulling the election's outcome and the country's political divide," the *New York Times* explained.[26] Trump's uneven performance as president and the questionable conduct of some of his family members, aides, appointees, and supporters have attracted a high level of scrutiny from the media. Trump's controversial political agenda has also created many issues for journalists to investigate, particularly given the president's propensity to change his stance on issues as he confronts them.[27] The fact that so many journalists are liberal Democrats and disagree with the president politically, and that Trump has angered reporters with his Nixonian attacks against the media, has likely added even more urgency to reporters' desire to perform the watchdog role over the Trump administration. "You have forced us to rethink the most fundamental questions about who we are and what we are here for," wrote the editor of *Columbia Journalism Review* in an open letter to the president. "For that we are most grateful."[28] As this book goes to press in 2017, I certainly believe I am seeing even more deep watchdog reporting than ever as I read the nation's newspapers.

However, a discussion about quantity alone is not sufficient to assess fully the outlook for accountability journalism. It is also a question of complexity. I suspect that newspaper reporters have become better able to dig into complex stories using new digital tools since 2011, as a cadre of specialists trained specifically to produce data journalism has started to appear in newsrooms with more tools than ever at their disposal. These digital tools are helping reporters gather, analyze, and present interactive information like never before. As an example, consider the *Atlanta Journal-Constitution*'s spectacular 2016 investigation into how doctors have gotten away with sexually abusing their patients. The five-part series presented numerous examples of doctors who sexually abused patients and faced no punishment—driving their victims into self-doubt, depression, and even suicide:

> Society condemns sexual misconduct by most citizens and demands punishment. . . . But when a physician is the perpetrator, the *AJC* found, the nation often looks the other way. . . . The *AJC* is exposing a phenomenon of physician sexual misconduct that is tolerated—to one degree or another— in every state in the nation.[29]

After noticing this trend in Georgia while looking into another story, the project team slowly expanded its investigation into all fifty states. To do so required adding all sorts of specialists. These included not only the kinds of computer programmers and specialists in data visualization who are typically being hired by newspapers as they move into data journalism, but also legal researchers and data scientists trained in artificial intelligence who "wrote computer programs to 'crawl' regulators' websites—a process known as scraping—and obtain [medical] board orders. This required building about 50 such programs tailored to agencies across the country."[30] Nearly fifty people are listed as having contributed to the *AJC*'s doctors series. The series won a boatload of awards and was even a finalist (meaning one of the two runners-up) for the 2017 Pulitzer Prize for National Reporting.[31] The impact of the series on those who were abused, or will not be because the issue has been exposed, is immeasurable.

Moving forward, there are reasons to believe that artificial intelligence, more commonly now called machine learning or deep learning, will have even larger effects on the production of accountability reporting over the coming decade. A twenty-three-page report by the Associated Press outlines how "augmented journalism" is likely to make reporting much easier in the not-so-distant future:

> Machine intelligence will be able to do much more than churn out straightforward, automated news reports. AI [artificial intelligence] will allow reporters to analyze data; identify patterns and trends from multiple sources; see things that the naked eye can't see; turn data and spoken words into text; text into audio and video; understand sentiment; analyze scenes for objects, faces, text, or colors—and more.[32]

The authors argue that leaning more on computers for basic journalistic functions frees up resources for stories that require more human capital, like accountability journalism. "The Associated Press began using algorithms to produce automated earnings reports in 2014 and estimates that doing so has freed up 20 percent of journalists' time, allowing those reporters to engage in more complex and qualitative work," the report says.[33] It goes on to quote Lisa Gibbs, AP's global business editor, who explained, "With the freed-up time, AP journalists are able to engage with more user-generated content, develop multimedia reports, pursue investigative work and focus on more complex stories."[34] Although the idea of computers churning out copy sounds troubling at first, I believe those who say that artificial intelligence is good, not bad, for news organizations. By making it easier to gather, analyze, and present information, augmented journalism would seem to bode well for those of us who care deeply about the watchdog function.

But all the technology in the world won't help if editors and publishers don't remain committed to fulfilling the watchdog role and to spending the money on reporters and the technology that enables them to dig. And editors' commitment will mean nothing without committed readers who pay for content in order to keep the press strong. Nothing would make me happier than to replicate my study for 2021 and see that the watchdog press continues to bark more loudly than ever. My hope is that this study will remind editors and reporters of the critically important role played by newspapers today. Even more importantly, I hope this research reminds the American people that they must consume news and be willing to pay for it in some way in order to make sure that accountability journalism continues to be provided. As the *New York Times* says in an advertising campaign that began just after Trump's inauguration, "The truth is more important now than ever."[35]

ACKNOWLEDGMENTS

I have truly been blessed to serve on the faculty of the Department of Communication and Media Studies at Fordham University. I thank each and every one of my colleagues for their support of this project and for countless kindnesses over the past years but extend particular thanks to former chairs Paul Levinson and James VanOosting and former acting chair Frederick Wertz. Special thanks to our dynamic and remarkable current chair, Dr. Jacqueline Reich, for her steadfast support of this book and of my career in general. I am also indebted to our department for research funds that helped fund the research and indexing of this book.

Thanks also to a few departmental colleagues: Professor Arthur S. Hayes, who offered invaluable advice throughout; Professors Margaret Schwartz and Jennifer Clark, who shared valuable insights during meetings of our writing group; Professor Amy Aronson, for her spot-on analysis of the early chapters; Professors Robin Andersen, Jessica Baldwin-Philippi, and Thomas McCourt, all directors of our graduate program, who helped me engage students in the research; Dr. Lewis Freeman, for his help with contacts; Mathias Klang for the useful advice on proofreading; and my "sister" associate chair at Fordham's Lincoln Center campus, Dr. Gwenyth Jackaway, for her moral support. Professor Jeffrey Cohen of Fordham's Department of Political Science also provided helpful advice on the data collection.

Former Fordham College at Rose Hill Dean Michael Latham and former Assistant Dean Michelle Bata provided grants to pay for undergraduates to help with the data collection, making a huge contribution to this work. John Harrington, former Dean of Arts and Sciences at Fordham, and Dr. Nancy Busch, former dean of Fordham's Graduate School of Arts and Sciences, also graciously supported this work with research grants. I am also most grateful for the ongoing support and friendship of Fordham's provost, Dr. Stephen Freedman. Thanks also to Fordham College at Rose Hill's wonderful current dean, Maura Mast, and her wonderful team of class deans and support staff.

Several other professors offered useful help and advice along the way: Professor Thomas Patterson of the Shorenstein Center on the Press, Politics and Public Policy at my alma mater, Harvard University's John F. Kennedy School of Government; Silvio Waisbord at George Washington University, who set a high bar with his work on watchdog journalism; Dr. Jonathan Gray, who basically taught me how to be a professor before he left Fordham for Wisconsin; and Zvi Reich, Professor at Ben-Gurion University of the Negev in Israel. Special thanks to Dr. Michael X. Delli Carpini, dean of the Annenberg School for Communication at the University of Pennsylvania, who critiqued this research in midstream, and to his gracious special assistant, Kelly Fernandez. I also thank the dean of the Stony Brook University School of Journalism, Howard Schneider, and his faculty—particularly Dean Miller, former head of Stony Brook's Center for News Literacy—for their useful feedback on the research following my seminar there in November 2014. Deep thanks to Dr. Jonathan Sanders of Stony Brook, one of my main partners in crime going back to the CBS News Moscow Bureau, for being such a dear friend and collaborator. And profound thanks to Professor C. W. Anderson of the City University of New York's College of Staten Island, who helped shape this work greatly through his review of the manuscript and extremely constructive comments.

Thanks, too, to Lynn Parliman and Kira Haimovsky of Fordham's Walsh Family Library; Vickie Kenny and Norma Kimbrough of Fordham's Graduate School of Arts and Sciences; our student assistants Amy Snopek and Zorana Vulevic; our wonderful departmental staff: Michelle O'Dwyer, Marie Trombetta, Claudia Rivera, and Roberta Palmerio; my former student Thomas Boscia and his mother, Dominique Boscia, for help with the *Bradenton Herald*; Madison Asplund and Karla McCann for help with the *Lewiston Tribune*; and the Association for Education in Journalism and Mass Communication (AEJMC), its director, Jennifer McGill, and project manager, Lillian Coleman, for supporting this work with an "emerging scholar" grant in 2013.

Sincere thanks go to the current and former editors who graciously spoke with me for the book, and whose input has made it a far better text: Doug Bauer, Joan Krauter, Joseph Lelyveld, Greg Moore, Kevin Riley, Rex Smith, Paul Steiger, Marty Baron, and my brothers-in-arms from the *Columbia Daily Spectator*, Marcus Brauchli and Duchesne Drew. Former editor of the *Cleveland Plain Dealer* Deborah Simmons was a great source of information. Charles Eisendrath, Lynette Clemetson, and Melissa Riley of the Livingston Awards provided invaluable assistance by including me at their annual luncheon.

Deep thanks to Professor Philip Napoli, formerly at Fordham but now at Duke University, whose keen eye and deep intelligence made him the ideal editor to bring this research into being; to Dr. Alice Marwick, former director of the Donald McGannon Communication Research Center at Fordham, for her support of making this work part of the Center's Everett C. Parker Book Series; and to Fredric Nachbaur, director of Fordham University Press, Eric Newman, its managing editor, and William Cerbone, its editorial associate, who have made me happy to be playing for the "home team." As always, Doug Grad, my agent and friend since we were fourteen, was a source of good advice and sage counsel, even if academic books don't make any money.

My special enthusiastic thanks go to my team of research assistants, who did the painstaking work of data collection: Fordham undergraduates Michael Broccolo, Erin Cavoto, Megan Falcone, Alyssa Fiorentino, Taylor Garre, Katherine Garrity, Nicholle Garzon, Donovan Longo, Megan McDonald, Elizabeth Ponce de Leon, Connor Ryan, Christopher Stevenson, and graduate students Paul Lauricella, Jesse Rabinowitz, and Timothy Vaughn. You each made a real contribution to this book, and I hope you will be proud of what we have discovered.

A few close friends were cheerleaders and pillars of support during the writing and research of this book: Diego Diaz, Lisa and Arieh Coll, Richard Froehlich and Joseph DiVito, Jennifer Eremeeva, Ira Gilbert, Susan Jane Gilman, Odette Walsh, Jessica Siegel, Mindy Siegel Ohringer, Caryn Rosenbaum and Glenn Wolff, Sushma Soni and Jeffrey Bartos, Alicia and James Weinstein, Katherine Dovlatov, Kathryn Calise and John Domville, David Fanger and Martin Wechsler, Domingo and Ayette Carrasco, Timothy Naftali, Peter Green and Babette Audant, Heidi Brown, Timothy McDarrah, Will Weinstein, Michelle Gittleman, Ari Mintz, Brandon Gauthier, Vlad Shamalov, and Sarah Wadsley. Special thanks to Kerry Abram and Elie Naufal for proofreading and improving the manuscript. Thanks as well to everyone in my extended Fierce Dragon Martial Arts family, with deepest gratitude to Master Michael Kimmel and Jessica

DeStefano Kimmel for teaching me the true meaning of indomitable spirit.

To Alex and Kirill Belyaninov, deep thanks for your endless support, and for putting up with the many months when I was totally engrossed in spreadsheets and article printouts. Alex, you remain the center of my world and my biggest inspiration. Thanks also to the rest of my family: Matthew Knobel; Mark, Raquel, Aaron, and Shaina Knobel; David, Trish, and Spencer Knobel; the Friedland, Schenker, and Davis families; the whole Fells clan; and my family members across the sea: Tamara Belyaninov, Gleb Belyaninov, and Svetlana Kocheeva. Thanks also to my "urban family" members: Priscilla Vazquez, Myrna Tarter, Seth Faulk, and Robert Pastore.

A giant thank you to my beloved partner, Dr. Thomas Masino, whose affection sustained me during the final push to publication.

Last, this book is dedicated to two men I have been most fortunate to have had in my life. The first is my mentor, Marvin Kalb, the great diplomatic correspondent for CBS and NBC News, author, and educator. In 1989, I landed on Marvin's doorstep, so to speak, as a doctoral student at Harvard, not long after he had arrived to lead the newly formed Shorenstein Center on the Press, Politics and Public Policy at the Kennedy School of Government. Since then he has enriched my life beyond words, as has his delightful and wise wife, Madeline. Marvin has not only taught me much about journalism, politics, and diplomacy, but he has also presented a model for living life as an honorable and righteous person. I am filled with gratitude to have fallen into Marvin's orbit and hope I have written a book that meets his very high standards. The second dedication is to my best friend, Dr. Mark Russell Shulman. Since we met at the salad bar at Columbia's John Jay Hall in 1981, Mark has been an unflagging supporter, confidante, and inspiration. More than thirty years later, I remain amazed and delighted that such an erudite and brilliant man has chosen this humble girl from Queens to be his closest pal. As I hosted a lunch for these two men as I was finishing this manuscript, I was reminded of how unspeakably lucky I have been to have them both in my corner.

NOTES

1. THE WATCHDOG STILL BARKS

1. See *Last Week Tonight*, Home Box Office, Aug. 7, 2016, retrieved at www.youtube.com/watch?v=bq2_wSsDwkQ.

2. Richard Paddock, Eric Lipton, Ellen Barry, Rod Nordland, Danny Hakim, and Simon Romero, "Potential Conflicts Around the Globe for Trump, the Businessman President," *New York Times*, Nov. 26, 2016, retrieved from www.nytimes.com/2016/11/26/us/politics/donald-trump-international-business.htm l?_r=0.

3. Bernard Condon, "Trump's tangled businesses pose potential for conflicts," *Detroit News*, Nov. 16, 2016, retrieved from www.detroitnews.com/story/news/nation/2016/11/16/trump-blind-trust/93963718/.

4. Paul Starr, "Goodbye to the Age of Newspapers (Hello to a New Era of Corruption)," *New Republic*, Mar. 4, 2009, retrieved from www.newrepublic.com/article/goodbye-the-age-newspapers-hello-new-era-corruption.

5. See David T.Z. Mindich, *Tuned Out: Why Americans Under 40 Don't Follow the News* (New York: Oxford University Press, 2004).

6. Newspaper Association of America figures, cited in David Collis, Peter Olson, and Mary Furey, "The Newspaper Industry in Crisis," Harvard Business School Case Study 9–709–463, May 22, 2009.

7. Economists do not agree about exactly when this financial crisis started. Some put it in 2008, but others say it begins as early as February 2007, when more than two dozen American subprime mortgage lenders went under.

For the sake of this work, I will use a start date of August 9, 2007, when European banks first suspended payments on funds backed by U.S. mortgage securities. See Stephen Cecchetti, "Monetary Policy and the Financial Crisis of 2007–2008," *Center for Economic Policy Research*, Apr. 3, 2008, retrieved from www.cepr.org/sites/default/files/policy_insights/PolicyInsight21.pdf.

8. Ibid.

9. Andrew Edgecliffe-Johnson, "Bleak outlook for US newspapers," *Financial Times*, Mar. 16, 2012, retrieved from www.ft.com/content/3eef0bc4 -6f73–11e1–9c57–00144feab49a.

10. Martin Baron, "Washington Post Editor Marty Baron Has a Message to Journalists in the Trump Era," *Vanity Fair*, Nov. 30, 2016, retrieved from www.vanityfair.com/news/2016/11/washington-post-editor-marty-baron -message-to-journalists.

11. John Nichols and Robert W. McChesney, "The Death and Life of Great American Newspapers," *The Nation*, Mar. 18, 2009, retrieved from www .thenation.com/article/death-and-life-great-american-newspapers/.

12. Author's discussion with Marvin Kalb, August 2009, quoted in Mike Wallace and Beth Knobel, *Heat and Light: Advice for the Next Generation of Journalists* (New York: Three Rivers Press, 2010), p. 10.

13. Jürgen Habermas (trans. Sara Lennox and Frank Lennox), "The Public Sphere—An Encyclopedia Article," *New German Critique*, No. 3 (Autumn 1974) pp. 49–55, retrieved from www.socpol.unimi.it/docenti/barisione/documenti/ File/2008–09/Habermas%20(1964)%20–%20The%20Public%20Sphere.pdf.

14. Ibid.

15. James Breig, "Early American Newspapering," *Colonial Williamsburg Journal*, Spring 2003, retrieved from www.history.org/Foundation/journal/ spring03/journalism.cfm.

16. Dean Starkman, "The Hamster Wheel," *Columbia Journalism Review*, Sept. 14, 2010, retrieved from www.cjr.org/cover_story/the_hamster_wheel.php ?page=all.

17. Laura Frank, "The Withering Watchdog, Part One," *PBS*, June 2009, retrieved from www.pbs.org/wnet/expose/2009/06/the-withering-watchdog.html.

18. Prior Markus, *Post-Broadcast Democracy: How Media Choice Increases Inequality in Political Involvement and Polarizes Elections* (New York: Cambridge University Press, 2007).

19. Annie Lang, Mija Shin, Samuel D. Bradley, Zheng Wang, Seungjo Lee, and Deborah Potter, "Wait! Don't Turn That Dial! More Excitement to Come! The Effects of Story Length and Production Pacing in Local Television News on Channel Changing Behavior and Information Processing in a Free Choice Environment," *Journal of Broadcasting & Electronic Media*, 49 (1), 2005, pp. 3–22.

20. Kiku Adatto, "Sound Bite Democracy—Network Evening News Presidential Campaign Coverage 1968 and 1988," Research paper R–2, Harvard

University, Joan Shorenstein Barone Center on the Press, Politics and Public Policy, June 1990; and Dean Starkman, "Major papers' longform meltdown," *Columbia Journalism Review*, Jan. 17, 2013, retrieved from www.cjr.org/the _audit/major_papers_longform_meltdown.php?page=all.

21. Adatto, "Sound Bite Democracy."

22. Stephen J. Farnsworth and Robert Lichter, *The Nightly News Nightmare: Media Coverage of U.S. Presidential Elections, 1988–2008*, 3d ed. (Lanham, Md.: Rowman and Littlefield, 2010).

23. See Prior, *Post-Broadcast Democracy* and Diana C. Mutz, "Effects of 'In-Your-Face' Television Discourse on Perceptions of a Legitimate Opposition," University of Nebraska, Hendricks Symposium, Department of Political Science, Paper 16, 2006, retrieved from digitalcommons.unl.edu/politicalscience hendricks/16.

24. James Q. Wilson, "How Divided Are We?" *Commentary*, Feb. 1, 2006, retrieved from www.commentarymagazine.com/article/how-divided-are-we/.

25. Nicholas Carr, *The Shallows: What the Internet Is Doing to Our Brains* (New York: Norton, 2011); and Matt Richtel, "Attached to Technology and Paying a Price," *New York Times*, June 6, 2010, retrieved from www.nytimes.com/ 2010/06/07/technology/07brain.html?pagewanted=all&_r=0.

26. Nichols and McChesney, "The Death and Life of Great American Newspapers."

27. Marisa Guthrie, "Investigative Journalism Under Fire," *Broadcasting & Cable*, June 23, 2008, retrieved from www.broadcastingcable.com/news/news -articles/investigative-journalism-under-fire/84851.

28. Jodi Enda, "Capital Flight," *American Journalism Review*, Summer 2010, retrieved from ajrarchive.org/article.asp?id=4877.

29. See, for example, C. W. Anderson, *Rebuilding the News: Metropolitan Journalism in the Digital Age* (Philadelphia: Temple University Press, 2013); David M. Ryfe, *Can Journalism Survive? An Inside Look at American Newsrooms* (Malden, Mass.: Polity, 2012); and Nikki Usher, *Making News at The New York Times* (Ann Arbor: University of Michigan Press, 2014).

30. See, for example, Dean Starkman, *The Watchdog That Didn't Bark: The Financial Crisis and the Disappearance of Investigative Journalism* (New York: Columbia University Press, 2014); Mitchell Stephens, *Beyond News: The Future of Journalism* (New York: Columbia University Press, 2014); Keith L. Herndon, *The Decline of the Daily Newspaper: How an American Institution Lost the Online Revolution* (New York: Peter Lang, 2012); Jeff Jarvis, *Geeks Bearing Gifts: Imagining New Futures for News* (New York: CUNY Journalism Press, 2014); Katherine Fink and Michael Schudson, "The Rise of Contextual Journalism, 1950s–2000s," *Journalism*, Jan. 2014, vol. 15, no. 1, pp. 3–20; and Ignacio Siles and Pablo J. Boczkowski, "Making sense of the newspaper crisis: A critical assessment of existing research and an agenda for future work," *New Media & Society*, Aug. 21, 2012.

31. Kevin Riley interview, July 10, 2015.

32. Duchesne Drew interview, May 31, 2014.

33. Doug Bauer interview, July 27, 2015.

34. According to data from the National Telecommunications and Information Agency, part of the Commerce Department, 32.8 percent of Americans were using the Internet at some location in December 1998—the first time the agency produced this kind of figure on Internet penetration. By Sept. 2001, that figure had topped 50 percent. See www.ntia.doc.gov/data/digital-nation -data-explorer#sel=internetUser&disp=map.

35. Although both Fox News Channel and MSNBC both launched in 1996, it is important to remember that MSNBC took on its very liberal character only after 2004 or so. During the Clinton–Lewinsky affair, MSNBC anchors and guests often were highly critical of President Bill Clinton.

36. Bruce A. Williams and Michael X. Delli Carpini, "Unchained Reaction: The collapse of media gatekeeping and the Clinton–Lewinsky scandal," *Journalism*, 2000 vol. 1, no. 1, p. 75, retrieved from pdfs.semanticscholar.org/ 29da/7b2e47156f088eeeffdeob141ea9541cf590.pdf.

37. See Larry J. Sabato, *Feeding Frenzy: Attack Journalism and American Politics* (Baltimore: Lanahan, 1991).

38. Robert Sherrill, "Examining the Vanishing Standards in Reporting, *Nieman Reports*, Mar. 15, 2002, retrieved from niemanreports.org/articles/ examining-the-vanishing-standards-in-reporting/.

39. Murrey Marder, "Arrogance Wins? American Journalism's Identity Crisis," *Nieman Reports*, Sept. 15, 1998, retrieved from http://niemanreports.org/ articles/arrogance-wins-american-journalisms-identity-crisis/.

40. As one *Washington Post* columnist put it, "There's no question that the Clinton–Lewinsky scandal—and by that I mean the whole thing, including how the media covered it, how politicians reacted to it and how technology turned into a worldwide sensation—was a pivot point in American politics, a time when things changed and haven't changed back." See Chris Cillizza, "How Monica Lewinsky Changed Politics," *Washington Post*, Oct. 20, 2014, retrieved from www.washingtonpost.com/news/the-fix/wp/2014/10/20/how -monica-lewinsky-changed-politics/?utm_term=.0c54e2cc2330.

41. Williams and Delli Carpini, "Unchained Reaction," p. 61.

42. The Audit Bureau of Circulation reported that while the Clinton– Lewinsky sex scandal was unfolding, nineteen of the top twenty-five newspapers reported gains in circulation, but the gains were short-lived. By mid-1999, after Clinton had been impeached and tried, thus quieting the scandal, newspaper circulation was down slightly overall. See adage.com/article/news/newspapers -disappointing-circulation-news-audit-bureau-reports-o-5-drop-naa-readies -marketing-push/62495/.

43. My research assistants and I also examined the output of the *NBC Nightly News*, *Time*, and *The New Yorker* from 1991 to 2011 and found limited

amounts of deep accountability reporting. I therefore have limited this book to newspaper coverage.

44. Greg Moore, e-mail with written answers to author's questions, July 13, 2015.

45. Rem Reider, "Amazing Enterprise Reporting," *American Journalism Review*, June/July 2012, retrieved from http://ajrarchive.org/article.asp?id=5284.

46. Moore e-mail, July 13, 2015.

47. Rex Smith interview, June 23, 2015.

48. James T. Hamilton, *Democracy's Detectives* (Cambridge, Mass.: Harvard University Press, 2016), p. 12.

49. See Farhad Manjoo, "You Won't Finish This Article," *Slate*, June 6, 2013, retrieved from www.slate.com/articles/technology/technology/2013/06/how_people_read_online_why_you_won_t_finish_this_article.html.

50. In the sample for 1991, coded story length was 1,286 words. In 2011, it was little changed at 1,270 words.

51. The data indicated that 57 percent of coded stories contained references to published or publicly available documents in the 1991 sample, dropping to 48 percent in the 2011 sample.

52. In its 2011 sample, about 60 percent of those quoted in coded stories in the *Bradenton Herald* were government officials. At the *Lewiston Tribune*, that figure was more than 70 percent.

53. To judge the complexity of the reporting, I created a "critique index" to reflect the breadth of the inquiry: whether it examined a systemic issue, a problem with a handful of individuals, or a problem with one individual. This index dropped by about one-quarter over the study period.

54. For example, previous studies by the Readership Institute at Northwestern University suggest that coverage of government affairs that "looks out for my civic and personal interests" is a key motivating factor for newspaper readers. See Readership Institute, "Reaching New Readers: Revolution, not Evolution," June 2004, retrieved from www.readership.org/new_readers/data/overview.pdf.

55. Joseph Bernt and Marilyn Greenwald, "Enterprise and Investigative Reporting in Metropolitan Newspapers: 1980 and 1995 Compared," in Joseph Bernt and Marilyn Greenwald, eds., *The Big Chill: Investigative Reporting in the Current Media Environment* (Ames: Iowa State University Press, 2000), pp. 51–80.

56. Silvio Waisbord, *Watchdog Journalism in South America* (New York: Columbia University Press, 2000).

57. David Bandurski and Martin Hala, *Investigative Journalism in China: Eight Cases in Chinese Watchdog Journalism* (Seattle: University of Washington Press, 2010).

58. Steve Davis and Emilie Davis, *Think Like an Editor: 50 Strategies for the Print and Digital World* (Boston: Cengage Learning, 2012).

59. Starr, "Goodbye to the Age of Newspapers."

60. Pew Research Center Journalism and Media Staff, "How News Happens," Pew Research Center, Jan. 11, 2010, retrieved from www.journalism.org/analysis_report/how_news_happens.

61. Ibid.

62. Nate Silver, "A Note to Our Readers on the Times Pay Model and the Economics of Reporting," www.nytimes.com, Mar. 21, 2011, retrieved from fivethirtyeight.blogs.nytimes.com/2011/03/24/a-note-to-our-readers-on-the-times-pay-model-and-the-economics-of-reporting.

63. I am indebted to Dean Howard Schneider of the Stony Brook University School of Journalism and his faculty for pointing out to me that newspapers often run more long, deep enterprise stories toward the end of the year, in order to meet award deadlines.

64. Michele Weldon, *Everyman News: The Changing American Front Page* (Columbia: University of Missouri Press, 2008), p. 2.

65. Joseph Lelyveld interview, July 31, 2015.

66. Moore e-mail, July 13, 2015.

67. Ben Smith III, "RITE OF SPRING: Tag deadline brings long lines," *Atlanta Journal-Constitution*, Apr. 30, 1996, p. A1.

68. W. Lance Bennett and William Serrin, "The Watchdog Role," in Geneva Overholser and Kathleen Hall Jamieson, eds., *Institutions of American Democracy: The Press* (New York: Oxford University Press, 2005), p. 169.

69. Corey Mitchell and Jane Friedmann, "State ignores teacher licensing violations: Regulators say it's too hard to enforce the rules. Some lawmakers want a tougher approach," *Minneapolis Star Tribune*, Apr. 10, 2011, p. A1.

70. Patricia Callahan and Scott Kilman, "Seeds of Doubt: Some Ingredients Are Genetically Modified, Despite Labels' Claims," *Wall Street Journal*, Apr. 5, 2001, p. A1.

2. BIGGER MEANS BETTER

1. In the 2013 George Polk Award competition, for example, the *New York Times* and the *Washington Post* each won three awards out of seventeen total. The Polk Awards cover broadcast and print, again suggesting the dominance of these two newspapers' reporting. See liu.edu/Polk/Articles/Past-Winners#2013.

2. See Nate Silver, "A Note to Our Readers on the Times Pay Model and the Economics of Reporting," nytimes.com, Mar. 21, 2011, retrieved from fivethirtyeight.blogs.nytimes.com/2011/03/24/a-note-to-our-reader s-on-the-times-pay-model-and-the-economics-of-reporting.

3. Abigail Edge, "Washington Post 'most popular' newspaper site on Twitter, www.journalism.co.uk, Jan. 10, 2014, retrieved from www.journalism.co.uk/news/the-washington-post-is-most-popular-us-newspaper-site-on-twitter/s2/a555550/. The data from the firm Searchmetrics found that in 2013, the number

of times per week that content from the newspapers drove tweets averaged 275,193 tweets per week at the *Washington Post*, 261,422 tweets per week at the *New York Times*, 149,960 tweets per week at *USA Today*, and 134,248 tweets at the *Wall Street Journal*.

4. Joseph Lelyveld interview, July 31, 2015.

5. Donna Shaw, "The Pulitzer Cartel," *American Journalism Review*, Nov./Dec. 2006, retrieved from www.ajr.org/article.asp?id=4186.

6. Author's calculations from www.pulitzer.org, and Shaw, "The Pulitzer Cartel."

7. Marcus Brauchli interview, July 17, 2015.

8. In the study years 1991, 1996, and 2001, the *Journal* published just five days a week. A Saturday edition of the *WSJ* was added in 2005 and is reflected in the study of April 2006 and 2011. The Sunday *Wall Street Journal* is not published as a standalone newspaper but as pages on personal finance that appear in other national newspapers. Therefore the content of those pages has been omitted from this analysis because there is no front page to analyze, and the Sunday content is not included in the *Journal*'s digital database.

9. See, for instance, Paul Harris, "America's most revered newspaper is latest to be hit by financial woes," *The Guardian*, Jan. 10, 2009, retrieved from www.theguardian.com/media/2009/jan/11/new-york-times-credit-crunch.

10. Dean Baquet, "Memo to Staff," reprinted in Margaret Sullivan, "Dean Baquet's Charting the Future Note to Times Staff," nytimes.com, Jan. 6, 2015, retrieved from publiceditor.blogs.nytimes.com/2015/01/06/dean-baquets-charting-the-future-note-to-times-staff/?_r=0.

11. The *New York Times* has been referred to as a "paper of record" since 1913, when it first started publishing an index. See Shannon E. Martin and Kathleen A. Hansen, *Newspapers of Record in a Digital Age: From Hot Type to Hot Link* (Westport, Conn.: Praeger, 1998), p. 7.

12. Dean Baquet, "Memo to Staff," reprinted in Benjamin Mulling, "The New York Times of the future is beginning to take shape," Poynter Institute, May 21, 2016, retrieved from www.poynter.org/2016/the-new-york-times-of-the-future-is-beginning-to-take-shape/413097/.

13. Scott Shane and Benjamin Weiser, "Judging Detainee Risk, Often with Flawed Evidence," *New York Times*, Apr. 25, 2011, p. A1.

14. David Cay Johnston, "Big Gain for Rich Seen in Tax Cuts," *New York Times*, Apr. 5, 2006, p. A1.

15. C. J. Chivers, "For Black Officers, Diversity Has Its Limits," *New York Times*, Apr. 2, 2001; and C. J. Chivers, "Alienation Is a Partner for Black Officers," *New York Times*, Apr. 3, 2001, p. A1.

16. See also Jane Fritsch and David Rohde's stories on legal aid lawyers, *New York Times*, Apr. 8–10, 2001, p. A1.

17. See, for example, David Kocieniewski, "Torricelli Pressed Hard to Help Big Donor Pursue Korean Deal," *New York Times*, Apr. 22, 2001, p. A1.

18. Gretchen Morgenson, "Outside Advice of Boss's Pay May Not Be So Independent," *New York Times*, Apr. 10, 2006, p. A1.

19. Lelyveld interview, July 31, 2015.

20. Ibid.

21. The New York Times, "THE MEDIA BUSINESS: Times Has Gain in Quarter But Profit Drop for the Year," *New York Times*, Feb. 11, 1992, retrieved from www.nytimes.com/1992/02/11/business/the-media-business-times-has-gain-in-quarter-but-profit-drop-for-the-year.html.

22. Lelyveld interview, July 31, 2015.

23. Ibid.

24. Tuck School of Business at Dartmouth, "New York Times Digital," case study no. 2–0006, 2007, retrieved from www.hbs.edu/faculty/Publication%20Files/20006_NYTDigital[1]_5e87d3e2–642b-457b-aa7b-b76f8e269f9f.pdf. The New York Times Company, owner of the *New York Times* newspaper, does not break out its earnings by division, so I can only extrapolate the financial health of the *Times* newspaper from that of the entire Times Company, which was far more diversified during the early study years than today.

25. Christine Haughney, "New York Times Company Sells Boston Globe," *New York Times*, Aug. 3, 2013, retrieved from www.nytimes.com/2013/08/04/business/media/new-york-times-company-sells-boston-globe.html?pagewanted=all&_r=0. The *Times* sold the *Globe* publishing group, including the *Worcester Telegram & Gazette*, in 2013 for just $70 million, which Haughney calls "a staggering drop in values."

26. See Sarah Ellison, "How a Money Manager Battled New York Times," *Wall Street Journal*, Mar. 21, 2007, retrieved from online.wsj.com/news/articles/SB117441975619343135.

27. Dylan, "New York Times to Reduce Size of Paper, Production Staff," *fishbowlny.com*, July 18, 2006, retrieved from www.mediabistro.com/fishbowlny/new-york-times-to-reduce-size-of-paper-production-staff_b2689.

28. Christine Haughney, "New York Times Seeks Buyouts from 30 in Newsroom," *New York Times*, Dec. 3, 2012, retrieved from mediadecoder.blogs.nytimes.com/2012/12/03/new-york-times-seeks-buyouts-from-30–newsroom-managers/?_php=true&_type=blogs&_r=0.

29. See, for example, Andres Martinez, "Slim's Pickings," *Slate.com*, Jan. 20, 2009, retrieved from www.slate.com/articles/news_and_politics/foreigners/2009/01/slims_pickings.html.

30. Michael Calderone, "New York Times Keeps Cutting Newsroom Jobs, but Headcount Doesn't Budge," *Huffington Post*, Oct. 8. 2014, retrieved from www.huffingtonpost.com/2014/10/08/new-york-times-buyouts-newsroom-headcount_n_5952646.html; and Lauren Indvik, "New York Times to Downsize Newsroom as Ad Revenue Falters," *Mashable*, Dec. 3, 2012, retrieved from mashable.com/2012/12/03/new-york-times-30-buyout/.

31. Peter H. Lewis, "New York Times Introduces a Web Site," *New York Times*, Jan. 22, 1996, retrieved from www.nytimes.com/1996/01/22/business/the -new-york-times-introduces-a-web-site.html.

32. Lelyveld interview, July 31, 2015.

33. Willa Frej, "The 'Failing' New York Times Just Hit a New Record for Subscriptions," huffpost.com, July 27, 2017, retrieved from http://www.huffing tonpost.com/entry/new-york-times-record-subscriptions_ us_5979e57fe4b02a4ebb734f5f.

34. Sydney Ember, "New York Times Co.'s Decline in Print Advertising Tempered by Digital Gains," *New York Times*, Feb. 2, 2017, retrieved from https:// www.nytimes.com/2017/02/02/business/media/new-york-times-q4-earnings .html?mcubz=0.

35. See Baquet, quoted in Sullivan, "Dean Baquet's Charting the Future Note to Times Staff."

36. For research on the role of national newspapers in agenda setting, see Maxwell McCombs and Donald Shaw, "The agenda-setting function of mass media," *Public Opinion Quarterly*, 36, 1972, pp. 176–87; and James W. Dearing and Everett M. Rogers, *Agenda-setting* (Thousand Oaks, Calif.: Sage, 1996).

37. Amber E. Boydstun, *Making the News: Politics, the Media, and Agenda Setting* (Chicago: University of Chicago Press, 2013), p. 11.

38. For more on the *NYT* ripple effect, see Stephen D. Reese and Lucig H. Danielian, "Intermedia influence and the drug issue: Converging on cocaine," in P. J. Shoemaker, ed., *Communication campaigns about drugs: Government, media, and the public* (Hillsdale, N.J.: Erlbaum, 1989), pp. 29–46; and Guy Golan, "Inter-Media Agenda Setting and Global News Coverage," *Journalism Studies*, vol. 7, no. 2, 2006, pp. 323–33.

39. Brauchli interview, July 17, 2015.

40. Joel Auerbach and Serge Kovaleski, "The Profile of a Loner," *Washington Post*, Apr. 7, 1996, p. A1.

41. Michael Abramowitz, "A Few Determined Men Made Stadium Dreams Come True," *Washington Post*, Apr. 14, 1996, p. A1.

42. Brauchli interview, July 17, 2015.

43. See Encyclopedia Britannica, "The Washington Post," retrieved from www.britannica.com/topic/The-Washington-Post.

44. Charles Babcock and Ann Devry, "Sununu Frequent Flier of Military Aircraft," *Washington Post*, Apr. 21, 1991, p. A1.

45. Susan Schmidt, "Bank Regulator Actively Trading," *Washington Post*, Apr. 30, 1991, p. A1.

46. Ruth Marcus, Walter Pincus, and Iran Chinoy, "Dole's Aggressive Maneuver: Spend Early and Freely," *Washington Post*, Apr. 18, 1996, p. A1.

47. Craig Whitlock, "Courted as Spies, Held as Combatants," *Washington Post*, Apr. 2, 2006, p. A1.

48. Thomas E. Ricks, "Military Plays Up Role of Zarqawi," *Washington Post*, Apr. 10, 2006, p. A1.

49. Joby Warrick, "An Outbreak Waiting to Happen," *Washington Post*, Apr. 9, 2001, p. A1.

50. Kirsten Downey Grimsley, "Fear on the Line at Mitsubishi," *Washington Post*, Apr. 29, 1996, p. A1.

51. Maria Glod, "Fairfax Success Masks Gap for Black Students," *Washington Post*, Apr. 14, 2006, p. A1.

52. Mary Pat Flaherty, "District Still Lacks Breath Alcohol Test," *Washington Post*, Apr. 11, 2011, p. A1.

53. Katherine Boo, "Work at Barry's Home Skirted Bid Process," *Washington Post*, Apr. 15, 1996, p. A1.

54. Florence Graves and Sara Kehaulani Goo, "Boeing Rules and Parts Bent, Whistle-Blowers Say," *Washington Post*, Apr. 17, 2006, p. A1.

55. Grimsley, "Fear on the Line at Mitsubishi."

56. The Washington Post Company, *IRS Form 10–K* (Annual Report), 1991–2012.

57. Kaplan's profits began to fall in light of increased federal scrutiny brought on, in part, by an investigation by the *New York Times*. See Tamar Lewin, "Scrutiny Takes Toll on For-Profit College Company," *New York Times*, Nov. 9, 2010, retrieved from www.nytimes.com/2010/11/10/education/10kaplan.html?_r=1&hp=&pagewanted=all.

58. Chris Kirkham, "Washington Post Co.'s Kaplan Bet May Have Cost It the Paper," *Huffington Post*, Aug. 6, 2013, retrieved from www.huffingtonpost.com/2013/08/06/washington-post-kaplan_n_3715396.html.

59. David Remnick, "Donald Graham's Choice," *The New Yorker*, Aug. 5, 2013, retrieved from www.newyorker.com/news/news-desk/donald-grahams-choice.

60. Michael Meyer, "Brick by Brick," *Columbia Journalism Review*, July/Aug. 2014, retrieved from www.cjr.org/cover_story/washington_post_jeff_bezos.php.

61. Gabriel Sherman, "Good News at the *Washington Post*," *New York*, June 28, 2016, retrieved from nymag.com/daily/intelligencer/2016/06/washington-post-jeff-bezos-donald-trump.html.

62. See the list of foreign correspondents, numbering twenty-two people in sixteen cities as of April 2017, at www.washingtonpost.com/news/world/washington-post-foreign-correspondents/?utm_term=.f2a81d3cc37c.

63. Quoted in Howard Kurtz, "Washington Post Shutters Last US Bureaus," *Washington Post*, Nov. 24, 2009, retrieved from www.washingtonpost.com/wp-dyn/content/article/2009/11/24/AR2009112403014.html.

64. Ibid.

65. Brauchli interview, July 17, 2015.

66. Ibid.

67. Ibid.

68. Keach Hagey, "Washington Post to close all but two local bureaus," *Politico*, Sept. 1, 2011, retrieved from www.politico.com/blogs/onmedia/0911/ Washington_Post_to_close_all_but_two_local_bureaus.html.

69. Brauchli interview, July 17, 2015.

70. Rachel Smolkin, "Reversing the Slide," *American Journalism Review*, Apr./May 2005, retrieved from ajrarchive.org/article.asp?id=3853.

71. Circulation in 2016 was about 390,000 daily and 580,000 on Sundays, according to the *Post*'s ad rate card. See washingtonpostads.com/sites/default/ files/15–1190–01.General.pdf.

72. Sherman, "Good News at the Washington Post."

73. Emily Steel, "Washington Post widens access to its digital content," *Financial Times*, Mar. 18, 2014, retrieved from www.ft.com/intl/ cms/s/0/4259186e-ae90–11e3–8e41–00144feab7de.html#axzz32MD4Iezh.

74. Joseph Lichterman, "The Washington Post goes national by offering free digital access to readers of local newspapers," *Nieman Lab*, Mar. 18, 2014, retrieved from www.niemanlab.org/2014/03/the-washington-post-goes-national -by-offering-free-digital-access-to-readers-of-local-newspapers/.

75. Justin Ellis, "By building partnerships with other newspapers, The Washington Post is opening up revenue opportunities," *Nieman Lab*, Apr. 7, 2015, retrieved from www.niemanlab.org/2015/04/congratulations-toledo-blade -reader-on-your-subscription-to-the-washington-post/.

76. Ibid.

77. Cynthia Crossen, "It All Began in the Basement of a Candy Store," *Wall Street Journal*, Aug. 1, 2007, retrieved from online.wsj.com/news/articles/ SB118591182345183718.

78. PressGazette, "Wall Street Journal most influential title among US financial journalists," Mar. 28, 2014, *PressGazette*, retrieved from www.press gazette.co.uk/content/wall-street-journal-most-influential-title-among-us -financial-journalists.

79. Ibid.

80. *Wall Street Journal*, Media Kit, retrieved from www.wsjmediakit.com/ newspaper.

81. Frank Ahrens, "Murdoch Seizes Wall St. Journal in $5 Billion Coup," *Washington Post*, Aug. 1, 2007, retrieved from www.washingtonpost.com/wp -dyn/content/article/2007/07/31/AR2007073100896.html.

82. Barry Ritholtz, "Murdoch's WSJ Changes Creates Opening for NYT, FT," *ritholtz.com*, Apr. 24, 2008, retrieved from ritholtz.com/2008/04/murdochs -wsj-changes-creates-opening-for-nyt-ft/.

83. See Mark Bowden, "Mr. Murdoch Goes to War," *The Atlantic*, July/ Aug. 2008, retrieved from www.theatlantic.com/magazine/archive/2008/07/mr -murdoch-goes-to-war/306867/.

84. Robert Bartley, "The Journal's Genius: Barney Kilgore Built His Vision," *Wall Street Journal*, June 23, 1989.

85. Brauchli interview, July 17, 2015.

86. Brauchli interview, July 17, 2015; and Dean Starkman, "The Winkler Way—Okay?" *Columbia Journalism Review*, June 3, 2008, retrieved from www .cjr.org/the_audit/the_winkler_wayokay.php?page=all.

87. Ralph T. King, "How Drug Firm Paid for Study by University, Then Yanked It," *Wall Street Journal*, Apr. 25, 1996, p. A1.

88. Guy Chazan and Gregory White, "Kremlin Connection Fails to Save BP from Oligarchs," *Wall Street Journal*, Apr. 11, 2011, p. A1.

89. Jim Carlton, "Oil and Ice: In Alaskan Wilderness, 'Friendlier Technology' Gets a Cold Reception—BP Amoco Workers Question Safety of Drilling Systems Bush Touts for Refuge—Firm Defends Pioneering Rigs," *Wall Street Journal*, Apr. 13, 2001, p. A1.

90. John Fialka, "Backfire: How Mercury Rules Designed for Safety End Up Polluting; Recycled in U.S., the Metal Journeys to Brazil's Jungles Where Gold Miners Burn It; A Murky Network of Brokers," *Wall Street Journal*, Apr. 20, 2006, p. A1.

91. Patricia Callahan and Scott Kilman, "Seeds of Doubt: Some Ingredients Are Genetically Modified, Despite Labels' Claims," *Wall Street Journal*, April 5, 2001, p. A1.

92. Dion Nissenbaum and Maria Abi-Habib, "Inside the Massacre at Afghan Compound," *Wall Street Journal*, Apr. 4, 2011, p. A1.

93. Ibid.

94. John R. Wilke, "Lawmaker Bought Farm with CEO Who Gained from Appropriations," *Wall Street Journal*, Apr. 25, 2006, p. A1.

95. Brody Mullins, Susan Pulliam, and Steve Eder, "Financiers Switch to GOP," *Wall Street Journal*, Apr. 26, 2011, p A1.

96. Jerry Guidera, "Air and Water: FAA Tests Put Cloud over Cessna's Revival of Single Engine Line," *Wall Street Journal*, Apr. 30, 200, p. A1.

97. Robert Block and Jay Solomon, "Pentagon Steps up Intelligence Efforts inside U.S. Borders," *Wall Street Journal*, Apr. 27, 2006, p. A1.

98. Audit Bureau of Circulation figures, gathered by the author from various news sources.

99. Ibid.

100. Angelica LaVito, "News Corp beats earnings expectations, misses on revenue," cnbc.com, Aug. 10, 2017, retrieved from https://www.cnbc.com/2017/08/10/news-corp-earnings-q4–2017.html?view=story&%24DEVICE%24=native-android-tablet.

101. Bowden, "Mr. Murdoch Goes to War."

102. David McKnight, "Rupert Murdoch's News Corporation: A Media Institution with a Mission," *Historical Journal of Film, Radio and Television*, vol.

30, no. 3, Sept. 2010, p. 307, retrieved from http://www.tandfonline.com/doi/abs/10.1080/01439685.2010.505021?src=recsys&journalCode=chjf20.

103. Quoted in Alicia Shepard, "Anonymous Sources," *Columbia Journalism Review*, Dec. 1994, retrieved from ajrarchive.org/article.asp?id=1596.

104. For an excellent comprehensive discussion of anonymous sources, see Matt Carlson, *On the Condition of Anonymity: Unnamed Sources and the Battle for Journalism* (Urbana: University of Illinois Press, 2011).

105. See the Associated Press News Editors survey quoted in Ryan Pitts, "Readers: Anonymous Sources Affect Media Credibility," *Poynter Institute*, June 16, 2005, retrieved from www.poynter.org/2005/readers-anonymous-sources-affect-media-credibility/69577/.

106. See Dean Baquet, Matt Purdy, and Phil Corbett, "A Note from Dean Baquet, Matt Purdy and Phil Corbett: New Guidelines of Anonymous Sources," nytco.com, Mar. 15, 2016, retrieved from http://www.nytco.com/a-note-from-dean-baquet-matt-purdy-and-phil-corbett-new-guidelines-on-anonymous-sourcing/.

107. Andrew Alexander, "For the Post, anonymous sources remain a problem," *Washington Post*, June 13, 2010, retrieved from www.washingtonpost.com/wp-dyn/content/article/2010/06/11/AR2010061104313.html.

3. THE WORKHORSE OF THE WATCHDOGS

1. My conclusions are based on an examination of all front-page stories for the months of April in 1991, 1996, 2001, 2006, and 2011 in the four newspapers. A total of 2,068 stories were examined—653 stories in the *AJC*, 523 in the *StarTrib*, 480 in the *Denver Post*, and in 412 the *Times Union*.

2. Kevin Riley interview, July 10, 2015.

3. Thomas Wheatley, "AJC staffers told layoffs are possible," *Creative Loafing Atlanta*, Sept. 18, 2013, retrieved from clatl.com/freshloaf/archives/2013/09/18/ajc-staffers-told-that-layoffs-are-possible; and Carl Sessions Stepp, "Transforming the Architecture," *American Journalism Review*, Oct./Nov. 2007, retrieved from ajrarchive.org/Article.asp?id=4402.

4. E-mail from Duchesne Drew, Oct. 5, 2013.

5. See Aldo Svaldi, "Post plans to reduce newsroom staff by 25," *Denver Post*, Apr. 19, 2006, retrieved from www.denverpost.com/business/ci_3725063; and Michael Roberts, "Denver Post layoffs estimate: 16 copy editors, nearly tenth of staff," *Westword*, May 2, 2012, retrieved from blogs.westword.com/latestword/2012/05/denver_post_copy_editing_layoffs_newspaper_guild_objects.php.

6. Rachel Templeton, "Charting a Course for Change: Transforming the Albany Times Union in a Wired World," Knight Case Studies Initiative, Graduate School of Journalism, Columbia University, 2007, p. 3, retrieved

from ravencommunications.com/pdfs/case_studies/knight_timesunion.pdf; and Rex Smith interview, June 23, 2015.

7. Sources for this short history of the *Atlanta Journal-Constitution* include the paper's own website; Chuck Perry, "Atlanta Journal-Constitution," *New Georgia Encyclopedia*, Jan. 5, 2004, retrieved from www.georgiaencyclopedia.org/articles/arts-culture/atlanta-journal-constitution; and Margaret Mitchell and Patrick Allen, *Margaret Mitchell: Reporter* (Athens, Ga.: Hill Street Press, 2000).

8. Stepp, "Transforming the Architecture."

9. Ibid.

10. Julia Klein, "If You Build It . . . " *Columbia Journalism Review*, Nov./Dec. 2007, retrieved from www.cjr.org/feature/if_you_build_it.php?page=all.

11. Butch Ward, "Watchdog Culture: Why You Need It, How You Build It," *Poynter Institute*, May 26, 2005, retrieved from www.poynter.org/how-tos/leadership-management/what-great-bosses-know/67742/watchdog-culture-why-you-need-it-how-you-can-build-it/.

12. Amy Chown, "Reader-driven improvements bring circulation gains to Atlanta-Journal Constitution," *International News Media Association*, July 1, 2012, retrieved from www.inma.org/article/index.cfm/56026-reader-driven-improvements-bring-circulation-gains-to-atlanta-journal-constitution.

13. Riley interview, July 10, 2015.

14. Tim Eberly, "Fast profit made off Gwinnett schools," *Atlanta Journal-Constitution*, Apr. 3, 2011, p. 1A.

15. Jaime Sarrio, "Minorities struggle in finalists' districts," *Atlanta Journal-Constitution*, Apr. 8, 2011, p. 1A.

16. See, for example, James Salzer, "Who gets what is top secret," *Atlanta Journal-Constitution*, Apr. 3, 2011, p. 1A. The story explains that Salzer "has been covering state politics and finance at the Georgia Capitol for more than 20 years, including the past 11 years for The Atlanta Journal-Constitution. Salzer currently serves as a Sunday watchdog reporter at the statehouse specializing in how state government raises as spends your money."

17. Chris Joyner and Aaron Gould Shinin, "Big tab wining, dining Capitol," *Atlanta Journal-Constitution*, Apr. 24, 2011, p. 1A.

18. Alison Young, "Eye-care plant uninspected since '03," *Atlanta Journal-Constitution*, Apr. 19, 2006, p. 1A.

19. Riley interview, July 10, 2015.

20. M. B. Pell, "Hospital bills may add pain," *Atlanta Journal-Constitution*, Apr. 17, 2011, p. 1A.

21. Heather Vogell, "Private agency, public power," *Atlanta Journal-Constitution*, Apr. 10, 2011, p. 1A.

22. See www.bizjournals.com/atlanta/news/2013/05/06/georgia-up-to-16-companies-on-fortune.html.

23. Scott Henry, "Newsroom musical chairs at the AJC," *Creative Loafing Atlanta*, Apr. 18, 2007, retrieved from clatl.com/atlanta/newsroom-musical-chairs-at-the-ajc/Content?oid; eq1266923.

24. Ken Edelstein, "AJC staff cuts harsher this time," *Creative Loafing Atlanta*, July 16, 2008, retrieved from clatl.com/freshloaf/archives/2008/07/16/ajc-staff-cuts-harsher-this-time.

25. Quoted in press release, July 16, 2008, reprinted by *Creative Loafing Atlanta*, retrieved from clatl.com/freshloaf/archives/2008/07/16/ajc-announces-cuts-of-180/.

26. Michael Joseph, "The AJC is optimistic on what the future holds," *Atlanta Journal-Constitution*, Dec. 26, 2010, p. A21.

27. Jim Romanesko, "Cox Media papers to consolidate copy editing, other jobs," *Poynter Institute*, Oct. 28, 2011, retrieved from www.poynter.org/latest-news/mediawire/151303/cox-media-papers-to-consolidate-copy-editing-other-jobs/.

28. Riley interview, July 10, 2015.

29. Atlanta Business Chronicle, "AJC publisher John Mellott retiring," *Atlanta Business Chronicle*, Jan. 12, 2009, retrieved from www.bizjournals.com/atlanta/stories/2009/01/12/daily5.html?page=all.

30. Riley interview, July 10, 2015.

31. Alliance for Audited Media figures.

32. Ibid.

33. Although he was serving as managing editor of the *Star Tribune* when interiewed for this book, Drew subsequently left the paper. Since March 2015, Drew has served as Community Network Vice President at the Bush Foundation, a community-focused NGO serving Minnesota, North Dakota, South Dakota, and twenty-three native communities located in those states.

34. Duchesne Drew interview, May 31, 2014.

35. *Star Tribune*, press release, Sept. 18, 2013, retrieved from www.Startribunecompany.com/learn-about-us/news/press-release/star-tribune-announces-departure-of-nancy-barnes-editor-and-senior-vice-president-after-distinguished-10-year-tenure-marked-by-award-winning-journalism/.

36. *Minneapolis Star Tribune*, "Chat on Oct. 22, 2013: Ask the Editor Rene Sanchez," *startribune.com*, Oct. 22, 2013, retrieved from live.startribune.com/Event/Live_chat_at_noon_Tuesday_As k_the_Editor_Rene_Sanchez.

37. Alliance for Audited Media figures.

38. Mark Lisheron, "Star Tribulation," *American Journalism Review*, Aug./Sept. 2007, retrieved from ajrarchive.org/article.asp?id=4382.

39. See the excellent interactive graphics at www.minnpost.com/braublog/2012/10/mapping-newspaper-war-25-years-after-star-tribune-invaded-pioneer-press-turf.

40. Associated Press, "Star Tribune cutting newsroom staff, increasing suburban coverage," *Winona Daily News*, May 16, 2007, retrieved from www .winonadailynews.com/news/state-and-regional/mn/star-tribune-cutting -newsroom-staff-increasing-suburban-coverage/article_ed787dd7–e8c0–59a4 –9b21–22fd606f1447.html.

41. Drew interview, May 31, 2014.

42. Ibid.

43. Robert Whereatt, "Ventura's troopers rake in overtime," *Star Tribune*, Apr. 18, 2001, p. A1.

44. Corey Mitchell and Jane Friedmann, "State ignores teacher licensing violations," *Star Tribune*, Apr. 10, 2011, p. A1.

45. Mike Kaszuba and Laurie Blake, "A vision clouded," *Star Tribune*, Apr. 14, 1991, p. A1.

46. See, for example, Chris Serres and Patrick Kennedy, "Executive Perks Are Piling Up: There's Chauffeuring, Country Club Memberships and More," *Star Tribune*, Apr. 3, 2011; and David Shaffer, "Salmonella Rates High at State Plants," *Star Tribune*, Apr. 14, 2006, p. 1A.

47. http://money.cnn.com/magazines/fortune/fortune500/2012/states/ MN.html.

48. Paul McEnroe, "Illegal Guns Flooding into Minneapolis," *Star Tribune*, Apr. 30, 2006, p. 1A; and David Chanen, "Williams' Trial in Vikings Case Begins Today," *Star Tribune*, Apr. 19, 2006, p. 1A.

49. Martha Sawyer, "For Some Ministers, Living by the Word Can be a Struggle," *Star Tribune*, Apr. 23, 1991, p. 1A.

50. Alliance for Audited Media figures.

51. Drew interview, May 31, 2014.

52. Moore was serving as editor when interviewed for this book. He resigned as editor of the *Denver Post* in March 2016.

53. Greg Moore, e-mail with written answers to author's questions, July 13, 2015.

54. Alicia C. Shepard, "Showdown in the Rockies," *American Journalism Review*, Oct. 1995, retrieved from http://ajrarchive.org/article.asp?id=1591.

55. Bob Burdick, "Remembering the Rocky," *Columbia Journalism Review*, Feb. 27, 2009, retrieved from www.cjr.org/behind_the_news/remembering_the _rocky.php?page=all.

56. Post-Intelligencer Staff, "12 cities still have JOAs," *Seattle Post-Intelligencer*, Apr. 28, 2003, retrieved from www.seattlepi.com/business/article/ 12-cities-still-have-JOAs-1113492.php.

57. Steve Raabe, "Economy, Internet whipsaw two-newspaper towns," *Denver Post*, Dec. 12, 2008, retrieved from www.denverpost.com/news/ci_11222657.

58. Robert Sanchez, "How Massive Cuts Have Remade the Denver Post," *5280 Magazine*, Sept. 2016, retrieved from www.5280.com/2016/09/how-massive

-cuts-have-remade-the-denver-post/. Exact figures on the *Post*'s digital circulation are not publicly available.

59. Figures from Greg Moore. Also see Svaldi, "Post plans to reduce newsroom staff by 25." In 2016, another round of cuts and buyouts took the staff down to about 100 overall. See Michael Roberts, "Denver Post seeks Buyout for 26, Would Reduce Newsroom by 1/3 in a year," *Westword*, Apr. 26, 2016, retrieved from http://www.westword.com/news/denver-post-seeks-buyout-for-26 -would-reduce-newsroom-by-1–3-in-a-year-7858385.

60. Michael Roberts, "Denver Post guilty of fuzzy math when touting circulation gains?" *Westword*, May 2, 2012, retrieved from blogs.westword.com/ latestword/2012/05/denver_post_fuzzy_math_circulation_gains_print.php.

61. Michael Roberts, "John Moore among 19 taking Denver Post buyouts, layoffs not expected," *Westword*, Nov. 30, 2011, retrieved from blogs.west word.com/latestword/2011/11/denver_post_buyouts_mike_keefe_joanne _davidson.php.

62. Moore e-mail, July 13, 2015.

63. See Mark Obmascik, "Flats sued, taxpayers pay," *Denver Post,* Apr. 7, 1996, p. A1.

64. See www.molsoncoors.com/en/our-story/our-history; ecorporateoffices .com/DishNetworkCorporation-1987; and www.fundinguniverse.com/company -histories/janus-capital-group-inc-history/.

65. Adreana Young, "Meet New Denver Post Editor Lee Ann Colacioppo," *Editor & Publisher*, Sept. 8, 2016, retrieved from www.editorandpublisher.com/ a-section/meet-new-denver-post-editor-lee-ann-colacioppo/.

66. Rex Smith interview, June 23, 2015.

67. Ibid.

68. Ibid.

69. The information for this history was taken from a *Times Union* article on its first 150 years, published Apr. 21, 2006, retrieved from extras.timesunion .com/tu150/index.html.

70. Paul Grondahl, "Big news, small time flavor," *Albany Times Union,* Aug. 21, 2006, retrieved from extras.timesunion.com/tu150/overview/overview4 .html.

71. Hearst profile, *Forbes*, retrieved from www.forbes.com/companies/ hearst/.

72. Templeton, "Charting a Course for Change," p. 2.

73. Smith interview, June 23, 2015.

74. Templeton, "Charting a Course for Change," p. 3.

75. Ibid., p. 6.

76. Figures provided by the Alliance for Audited Media, June 2014.

77. Templeton, "Charting a Course for Change," p. 5.

78. Ibid., p. 15.

79. Smith interview, June 23, 2015.

80. Templeton, "Charting a Course for Change," p. 13.

81. Ibid., p. 16.

82. *Albany Times Union* media kit, retrieved from web.timesunion.com/mediakit/. By August 2015, unique monthly visitors were up over 275,000. See timesuniondigital.com/internet-ads-in-albany-ny/.

83. See, for example, James M. Odato, "Funds followed senator's kin," *Albany Times Union*, Apr. 21, 2006, p. A1.

84. Tom Precious, "Bureaucrats play a shell game," *Albany Times Union*, Apr. 21, 1991, p. A1.

85. See, for example, Andrew Tilghman, "Culture of cars tests rail project," *Albany Times Union*, Apr. 29, 2001, p. A1.

86. See, for example, Brendan J. Lyons, "Cops bash DA, counsel breath test refusal," *Albany Times Union*, Apr. 14, 2011, p. A1.

87. Tom Precious, "Lawmakers want to ban lottery ads," *Albany Times Union*, Apr. 12, 1996, p. A1.

88. Matt Pacenza, "Hidden poison: MTBE Tainting water across state," *Albany Times Union*, Apr. 9, 2006, p. A1.

89. Theola S. Labbe, "Chief took 70 days on leave," *Albany Times Union*, Apr. 28, 2001, p. A1.

90. Smith interview, June 23, 2015.

91. Ibid.

92. The average number of words per accountability story fell from about 1,150 in the 2006 sample to 905 in 2011. The average number of people (sources) quoted per article at the *ATU* dropped from 5.1 in the 2006 sample to 3.9 in 2011.

93. I created an index to capture the complexity of the reporting, which fell at the *Times Union* from 2006 to 2011, indicating that accountability stories were moving toward examinations of wrongdoing involving just one or a few individuals rather than large-scale, systemic issues.

94. *Albany Times Union*, "TU+ Special Report: Toxic Risks," n.d., retrieved from www.timesunion.com/environment/.

95. Albany Times Union, "About the series," *Albany Times Union*, July 1, 2016, retrieved from www.timesunion.com/local/article/About-the-series-8334490.php.

96. MinnPost, "About Us," n.d., *MinnPost*, retrieved from www.minnpost.com/about.

97. Chris Benz, "MinnPost," n.d., *cjr.org*, retrieved from www.cjr.org/news_startups_guide/2011/01/minnpost.php.

4. AMERICA'S MOST VULNERABLE

1. Sandy Rowe, "Partners of Necessity: The Case for Collaboration in Local Investigative Reporting," Joan Shorenstein Center on the Press, Politics

and Public Policy Discussion Paper Series #D-62, June 2011, pp. 2–3, retrieved from shorensteincenter.org/wp-content/uploads/2012/03/d62_rowe.pdf.

2. Steven Waldman, et al., *The Information Needs of Communities*, Federal Communication Commission, 2011, p. 5, retrieved from transition.fcc.gov/osp/inc-report/The_Information_Needs_of_Communities.pdf.

3. Joan Krauter interview, July 31, 2015.

4. Doug Bauer interview, July 27, 2015.

5. See Jeff McGhee, "Rural Newspapers Doing Better Than Their City Counterparts," Stanford University Rural West Initiative, July 14, 2011, retrieved from web.stanford.edu/group/ruralwest/cgi-bin/drupal/content/rural-newspapers.

6. See www.mcclatchy.com.

7. See lmtribune.com. The paper was formerly known as the *Lewiston Morning Tribune*, hence the letter "m" in its web address.

8. Circulation and readership cited at www.bradenton.com/about-us/. The *Herald*'s readership, like that of all papers, is higher than its circulation; according to the paper, its June 2014 readership was 124,000 daily and 138,000 on Sundays. By September 2016, those readership figures had dropped to 107,000 daily and 131,000 Sunday.

9. The *Tribune* is not a member of the Alliance for Audited Media, as are the larger papers studied here. Circulation information comes from the *Tribune*'s managing editor, Doug Bauer.

10. That finding was suggested by changes to the index I created to measure whether stories were addressing a systemic issue or just a problem with an individual.

11. Nielsen estimate from 2015, calculated at www.tampabay.org/about-us/news-media/partnership-blog/2013–08–15/tampa-bays-population-growth-surpasses-growth-rate. U.S. census data gives similar figures.

12. The 65+ age group is the only one where newspaper readership still reaches 50 percent. See Pew Research Center, "Newspapers: Daily readership by age," *State of the News Media 2016*, retrieved from www.journalism.org/media-indicators/newspapers-daily-readership-by-age/.

13. Associated Press, "Tampa Bay Times Buys Rival, Tampa Tribune, and Begins to Close It Down," *New York Times*, May 3, 2016, retrieved from www.nytimes.com/2016/05/04/business/media/tampa-bay-times-buys-rival-tampa-tribune-and-starts-to-close-it-down.html.

14. The *Tampa Bay Times* website is www.tampabay.com. The *Herald* shares some content like state government coverage with the *Tampa Bay Times* and the *Miami Herald*, which, like the *Bradenton Herald*, is owned by the McClatchy Company. People who do not know Florida might think that the *Miami Herald* is the largest-circulation paper in Florida, but in fact the *Tampa Bay Times* has more than twice its circulation. See www.cision.com/us/2014/08/top-10-daily-newspapers-in-florida/ for the 2014 list of largest Florida newspapers.

15. The website for the *Sarasota Herald-Tribune* is www.heraldtribune.com.

16. U.S. Census Bureau, "Bradenton (city), Florida," n.d., retrieved from quickfacts.census.gov/qfd/states/12/1207950.html.

17. U.S. Census Bureau, "Manatee County, Florida," n.d., retrieved from www.census.gov/quickfacts/table/BZA210214/12081. Manatee County is middle-class (average household income is around $49,000) and 86 percent white, according to census data gathered between 2010 and 2015.

18. Krauter interview, July 31, 2015.

19. www.thebradentontimes.com.

20. www.bradenton.com/about-us/.

21. Krauter interview, July 31, 2015.

22. Ibid.

23. The McClatchy Company, *2014 Annual Report*, p. 2.

24. Krauter interview, July 31, 2015.

25. David Cox, "Legislator Accepts Funds from Source He Criticized," *Bradenton Herald*, Apr. 16, 1996, p. 1.

26. Duane Marsteller, "Manatee's Boot Camp in Trouble," *Bradenton Herald*, Apr. 2, 2006, p. 1.

27. Angeline Taylor, "Manatee school's health insurance runs $9.4M deficit," *Bradenton Herald*, Apr. 10, 2011, p. 1.

28. Duane Marsteller, "Bridge Contractor's Record Marred," *Bradenton Herald*, Apr. 1, 2001, p. 1.

29. Krauter interview, July 31, 2015.

30. Ibid.

31. The McClatchy Company, *Annual Report 2006*, released Mar. 1, 2007.

32. Noah David, "25 Newspapers That Have the Best Chance of Being Around in 10 Years," *Business Insider*, May 4, 2011, retrieved from www.business insider.com/top-25-newspapers-growth-los-angeles-times-roger-ebert-2011–5#ix zz1LlPeuHtn.

33. *Sarasota Herald-Tribune*, "Bradenton Herald parent posts $42 million profit," *Sarasota Herald-Tribune*, July 21, 2009, retrieved from www.heraldtribune .com/article/20090721/breaking/907219974?tc=ar.

34. Krauter interview, July 31, 2015.

35. Elaine Williams, "Alford Replaces Alford at Lewiston Tribune," *Lewiston Tribune*, October 2, 2008, retrieved from trib.com/news/state-and-regional/ alford-replaces-alford-at-lewiston-tribune/article_a824e632-7693-5756-b0c3 -1c654cbec39f.html.

36. Ibid.

37. *Lewiston Tribune*, "Lewiston Tribune Newspaper," *Facebook*, retrieved from www.facebook.com/lewistontribune/timeline.

38. Bauer interview, July 27, 2015. Bauer was at the time serving as managing editor of the *Tribune*. In May 2017, Bauer moved to the position of advertising director for the newspaper's parent, the Tribune Publishing Company.

39. Ibid.

40. *Lewiston Tribune*, "Lewiston Tribune Newspaper," *Facebook*, retrieved from www.facebook.com/lewistontribune?sk=info.

41. Bauer interview, July 27, 2015.

42. Williams, "Alford Replaces Alford at Lewiston Tribune."

43. U.S. Census Bureau, "Lewiston (city), Idaho," retrieved from www.census.gov/quickfacts/table/PST045216/1646540,12081.

44. U.S. Census Bureau "Nez Perce Country, Idaho," retrieved from factfinder.census.gov/faces/nav/jsf/pages/community_facts.xhtml?src=bkmk.

45. Quoted in Valdasue Steele, "A Guide to Living on the Nez Perce Reservation," University of Washington Extension, 2013, retrieved from www.aaanativearts.com/nez-perce/nez-perce-reservation.htm.

46. U.S. Census Bureau, "Table 1. Annual Estimates of the Population of Metropolitan and Micropolitan Statistical Areas: Apr. 1, 2010 to July 1, 2011," retrieved from https://www.census.gov/data/datasets/2016/demo/popest/total-metro-and-micro-statistical-areas.html.

47. Bauer interview, July 27, 2015.

48. Sandra L. Lee, "Bennett details troubles at former city job," *Lewiston Tribune*, Apr. 9, 2011, p 1.

49. Bauer interview, July 27, 2015.

50. Ibid.

51. Ibid.

5. IF NOT NOW, WHEN?

1. Richard Behar, "Open Letter to Russia's Putin on the Tenth Anniversary of Forbes Editor Paul Klebnikov's Murder: Why Haven't You Solved It?" *Forbes*, July 16, 2014, retrieved from www.forbes.com/sites/richardbehar/2014/07/16/open-letter-to-russias-putin-on-tenth-anniversary-of-forbes-editor-paul-klebnikovs-murder-why-havent-you-solved-this-case/.

2. Doug Bauer interview, July 27, 2015.

3. Paul Starr, "Goodbye to the Age of Newspapers (Hello to a New Era of Corruption)," *New Republic*, Mar. 4, 2009, retrieved from www.newrepublic.com/article/goodbye-the-age-newspapers-hello-new-era-corruption.

4. Steven Waldman, et al., *The Information Needs of Communities*, Federal Communication Commission, 2011, retrieved from transition.fcc.gov/osp/inc-report/The_Information_Needs_of_Communities.pdf.

5. Edward V. Murphy, "Who Regulates Whom and How? An Overview of U.S. Financial Regulatory Policy for Banking and Securities Markets," Congressional Research Service, May 28, 2013, pp. 2–3.

6. See Dean Starkman, *The Watchdog That Didn't Bark: The Financial Crisis and the Disappearance of Investigative Journalism* (New York: Columbia University Press, 2014).

7. Bureau of Labor Statistics Data, U.S. Department of Labor, cited in Terence P. Jeffrey, "Government Workers Now Outnumber Manufacturing Workers by 9,932,000," *CNS News*, Sept. 2, 2016, retrieved from www.cnsnews .com/news/article/terence-p-jeffrey/government-workers-now-outnumber -manufacturing-workers-9932000.

8. The percentage of businesspeople being quoted in the samples examined fell from a high of 13.6 in the 2001 sample to 7.6 in 2011.

9. See, for example, Craig Silverman, "This Analysis Shows How Fake Election News Stories Outperformed Real News on Facebook," *BuzzFeed*, Nov. 16, 2016, retrieved from www.buzzfeed.com/craigsilverman/viral-fake-election -news-outperformed-real-news-on-facebook?utm_term=.al5BGxbKW#.vnNY Go8Lg.

10. Jeff Jarvis, "Amid Constant Layoffs, Journalists Should Stop Parroting Each Other," *The Observer*, Aug. 12, 2015, retrieved from observer.com/2015/08/ amid-constant-layoff-journalists-should-stop-parroting-each-other/.

11. Alex Jones, *Losing the News: The Future of the News That Feeds Democracy* (New York: Oxford University Press, 2011).

12. Jarvis, "Amid Constant Layoffs."

13. Joel Simon, "Donald Trump Threatens Press Freedom Worldwide," *Columbia Journalism Review*, Oct. 13, 2016, retrieved from www.cjr.org/opinion/ trump_press_freedom.php?CJR.

14. Art Swift, "Americans' Trust in Mass Media Sinks to New Low," *Gallup*, Sept. 14, 2016, retrieved from www.gallup.com/poll/195542/americans-trust -mass-media-sinks-new-low.aspx.

15. Ibid.

16. Ibid.

17. For a brilliant graphic on how political polarization has increased in recent years, see "Political Polarization in the American Public," *Pew Research Center*, June 12, 2014, retrieved from www.people-press.org/2014/06/12/section-1 -growing-ideological-con sistency/#interactive.

18. This term, it must be said, did not result from Donald Trump's election but goes back at least to 2008. See Farhad Manjoo, *True Enough: Learning to Live in a Post-Fact Society* (Hoboken, N.J.: Wiley, 2008).

19. See Shannon Bond and David Bond, "Newspapers welcome more digital subscribers in time of fake news," *Financial Times*, Feb. 14, 2017, retrieved from www.ft.com/content/d97bef40-f19b-11e6-8758-687615182126.

20. Hillel, *Ethics of the Fathers (Pirkei Avot)*, 1:14.

21. Marcus Brauchli interview, July 17, 2015.

22. Sarah Smarsh, "What Donald Trump will have to accept: without journalism, there is no America," *The Guardian*, Nov. 18, 2016, retrieved from www .theguardian.com/media/2016/nov/18/american-media-journalism-donald-trump.

23. Robert Sanchez, "How Massive Cuts have Remade the Denver Post," *5280 Magazine*, Sept. 2016, retrieved from www.5280.com/2016/09/how-massive -cuts-have-remade-the-denver-post/.

24. Marty Baron interview, Apr. 27, 2017.

25. David Corn, "Trump, the Media, and You," *Mother Jones*, Mar. 16, 2016, retrieved from www.motherjones.com/media/2016/03/trump-the-media -and-you-3.

26. Nicholas Fandos,"Nonprofit Journalism Groups Are Gearing up With Flood of Donations," *New York Times*, Dec. 7, 2016, retrieved from www.nytimes .com/2016/12/07/business/media/nonprofit-journalism-groups-are-gearing-up-with -flood-of-donations.html?_r=0.

27. See Peter Baker, "For Trump, a Steep Learning Curve Leads to Policy Reversals," *New York Times*, Apr. 13, 2017, retrieved from www.nytimes.com/ 2017/04/13/us/politics/donald-trump-policy-revers als.html?_r=0.

28. Kyle Pope, "An open letter to Trump from the US press corps," *Columbia Journalism Review*, Jan. 17, 2017, retrieved from www.cjr.org/covering _trump/trump_white_house_press_corps.php.

29. Carrie Teegardin, Danny Robbins, Jeff Ernsthausen, and Ariel Hart, "License to betray," *Atlanta Journal-Constitution*, July 10, 2016, retrieved from doctors.ajc.com/doctors_sex_abuse/?ecmp=doctorssexabuse_microsite_nav.

30. *Atlanta Journal-Constitution*, "How the Doctors & Sex Abuse project came about," n.d., retrieved from doctors.ajc.com/about_this_investigation/.

31. See www.pulitzer.org/finalists/staff-187 and Lois Morder, "AJC inves- tigation wins national recognition," *Atlanta Journal-Constitution*, Apr. 6, 2017, retrieved from www.ajc.com/news/local/ajc-investigation-wins-national -recognition/m82z96okBxBvOyClPg9W1K/.

32. Francesco Marconi and Alex Siegman, "A day in the life of a journalist in 2027: Reporting meets AI," *Columbia Journalism Review*, Apr. 11, 2017, retrieved from www.cjr.org/innovations/artificial-intelligence-journalism.php.

33. Francesco Marconi, Alex Siegman, and Machine Journalist, *The Future of Augmented Journalism*, *Associated Press*, n.d., p. 4, retrieved from insights.ap .org/uploads/images/the-future-of-augmented-journalism_ap-report.pdf.

34. Ibid., p. 5.

35. Ann-Christine Diaz, 'The Truth Is Hard,' Says the New York Times' First-Ever Oscars Ad," *Ad Age*, Feb. 23, 2017, retrieved from adage.com/article/ advertising/truth-hard-york-times-oscars-ad/308069/.

INDEX

deep accountability reporting, 23, 65; enterprise journalism, 65; financial challenges, 55; focus on nongovernmental actors, 65–66; local focus, 62; prizes, 63; public service reporting, 65; simple enterprise stories, 27, 65; staff size, 64

Minnesota Public Radio, 79

MinnPost.com, 63, 79

Mitchell, Margaret, 57

Moore, Greg: on *The Denver Post*, 66, 69, 70; on focus on watchdog reporting, 11, 12; on front-page stories, 21

Moscow-Pullman Daily News, 90

Mother Jones, 111

MSNBC, 10

Murdoch, Rupert, 44–45, 52

NBC Nightly News, 17

The New Republic, 97

New York Times, 18; accountability reporting during 1991-2011, 33–34; acquisition and sale of the *Boston Globe*, 35–36; analysis of newspaper's original reporting, 17; anonymous sourcing, 52; author working at, 8; business strategy, 36–37; on challenges of covering Donald Trump's presidency, 2; circulation, 36; deep accountability reporting, 32, 35, 36, 50; digital readership, 36; and Donald Trump, 51; under editor Dean Baquet, 34–35; loan from Carlos Slim Helu, 36; number and percentage of deep accountability reports, 30–31, 32–37; as "paper of record", 32; prizes, 31, 32; revenues and profits, 35–36; simple enterprise stories, 27; staff size, 36; study of, 28–29; syndication of content, 37; visibility, 37

The New Yorker, 17

news aggregators, 13

News Corporation, 44–45, 49, 51

NewsLibrary (nl.newsbank.com), 18

newspaper industry: decline of, 2–3; watchdog reporting as a survival strategy, 14

newspapers: circulation figures, 2–3; as main drivers of investigative reporting, 16–17; paying for, 1–2; reasons to buy, 11–13

Nichols, John, 3, 7

nongovernmental focus: by the *Atlanta Journal-Constitution*, 60; by *The Denver Post*, 70; by the *Minneapolis Star Tribune*, 65–66; by the *Wall Street Journal*, 46–48

nonprofit journalism organizations, 108–9

NYT. See New York Times

Oliver, John, 1–2, 4

organizations studied, 17–20

paper of record, 32, 45

Parker, Penny, 68

Parkinson, Roger, 63

parroting coverage, 103

partnering with news nonprofits, 108–9

paying for content, 6

paywalls: at the *Albany* (New York) *Times Union*, 75, 77, 78; at the *Bradenton* (Florida) *Herald*, 86; at the *Lewiston* (Idaho) *Tribune*, 90; at the *Wall Street Journal*, 48–49; at the *Washington Post*, 43

Pew Research Center, Project for Excellence in Journalism, 16

Post. See Washington Post

post-factual society, 104–5

press freedom, Donald Trump as a threat to, 103–4

prestige, 14

prizes, 14, 29; won by the *Atlanta Journal-Constitution*, 112; won by *The Denver Post*, 67; won by the *Los Angeles Times*, 31; won by the

Philip M. Napoli and Minna Aslama, eds., *Communications Research in Action: Scholar-Activist Collaborations for a Democratic Public Sphere*

Kari Karppinen, *Rethinking Media Pluralism*

Richard D. Taylor and Amit M. Schejter, eds., *Beyond Broadband Access: Developing Data-Based Information Policy Strategies*

Des Freedman, Jonathan A. Obar, Cheryl Martens, and Robert W. McChesney, eds., *Strategies for Media Reform: International Perspectives*

Joshua D. Atkinson, *Journey into Social Activism: Qualitative Approaches*

Beth Knobel, *The Watchdog Still Barks: How Accountability Reporting Evolved for the Digital Age*